Care

Care

Judith Phillips

polity

First published in 2007 by Polity Press

Polity Press
65 Bridge Street
Cambridge CB2 1UR, UK

Polity Press
350 Main Street
Malden, MA 02148, USA

ISBN-13: 978-07456-2976-6
ISBN-13: 978-07456-2977-3 (pb)

A catalogue record for this book is available from the British Library.

Typeset in 10.5 on 12 pt Sabon
by SNP Best-set Typesetter Ltd., Hong Kong
Printed and bound in Great Britain
by MPG Printers Ltd, Bodmin, Cornwall

The publisher has used its best endeavours to ensure that the URLs for external websites referred to in this book are correct and active at the time of going to press. However, the publisher has no responsibility for the websites and can make no guarantee that a site will remain live or that the content is or will remain appropriate.

Every effort has been made to trace all copyright holders, but if any have been inadvertently overlooked the publisher will be pleased to include any necessary credits in any subsequent reprint or edition.

For further information on Polity, visit our website: www.polity.co.uk

Contents

1
An Introduction to Care

She was diagnosed with dementia so we got together and as
a family we decided you know, obviously it changed as time
went on but we sort of decided that we would literally give
our time to look after her in her own home.
Woman carer aged 45, in Phillips et al., 2002a

What is care? How would we recognize it? Who is a carer?
The above quote illustrates how we think about care and
how we often come across the concept – within a family
context. It is a term we frequently use, with a number of
meanings, conjuring up affection, love, duty, well-being,
responsibility and reciprocity. It is demonstrated through
touch, action, emotion and body expression. Care is fundamental to our individual identity as this is played out in our
social interactions and relationships. Care can be part of
formal, loving, professional and friendship relationships. It
is fundamental to who we are and how we are viewed in
both public and private spheres of life. It is often based on
a relationship, not only within a family context but with
others outside the family in a health or social care setting.
In many ways it is a nebulous and ambiguous concept and
a part of everyday life which is taken for granted.

At the same time care can be seen as a commodity or
product of a vast industry of service providers such as the

NHS, social services, housing and independent and voluntary sector agencies. Care demands considerable resources, organization and staffing. Within this setting it is regulated and formalized rather than spontaneous. Such organizations have a considerable impact on all of us at various times of life, particularly on those who are seen as 'vulnerable' in society, such as children, people with complex and multiple disabilities and older frail people. The importance of the concept of care has increasingly been acknowledged on both societal and individual levels. A society is often judged by the way it provides care. The principles of care are essential in understanding the context, legislation, policy and practices of the social and health services. Care is also the glue that binds individual relationships, as mentioned above.

The concept of care is framed by multifaceted argument and is subject to debate on a number of levels. Many of the current debates have a long history and evolution and include philosophical, ideological, political and economic arguments concerning the definition of care, who provides it, how and where it is provided and who provides funding. Some of the classic empirically based and theoretical studies on care (Finch and Mason, 1997; Finch and Groves, 1983; Nolan, Grant and Keady, 1996; Tronto, 1993; Bowlby, 1980) highlight questions of responsibility, burden, stress, care attachments, reward and ethics. These have been influential in raising the profile of care in policy and practice as well as academic debate worldwide.

It is the complexity of care that has made this concept one of relevance to a range of audiences. Over the last twenty years there has been heightened interest in caregiving from professionals and policy makers; yet this doesn't fully 'account for the concentration of work in this area by researchers representing multiple disciplines and theoretical orientations' (Pearlin, Piopli and McLaughlin, 2001). Anyone interested in the concept looking at the number of journal papers and academic conferences, articles in the popular press and in the media will be overwhelmed by attempts to quantify and define care. The central disciplines of social policy, sociology, social work, psychology, health, politics, philosophy, epidemiology and economics, among others, have attempted to grapple with the complexity of care.

Care is also characterized by diversity and 'multiple discourses' of caregiving (Gubrium, 1995) shaped by feminism, the disability movement, social policy analysts, legislators and carers' organizations. It is an evolving rather than a static concept through history and through the lifecourse and has different meanings depending on the cultural context. In the UK the care debate emerged as a result of academic and policy interest. At first it focused on carers, and then it broadened to take on a wider range of issues – the role of women, the nature of carework, the rights of disabled people and the effectiveness of community care (Twigg, 1998). As will be argued in the book, the notion of care in the twenty-first century has been recast – from the perception of care as a set of tasks, burdensome to the caregiver, to a broader perspective that views care within the wider environment in which it takes place, from duty and obligation to rights to give and receive care.

The way the language of care is used differs across child care and adult care. Social care is generally referred to when discussing adults. A distinction between child care and childcare (depending on a break between child and care) also exists. In this context the care debate has shifted historically from one around the public arena of care and children in the 'care system' (child care) to one where all care (childcare) that children receive draws attention.

The meaning of care can also differ depending on the viewing point – the differences for example between effective care and a caring person illustrate the point. A kind, well intentioned, loving person may be a very 'poor' carer, yet an adequate detached employee in the care sector may be an 'adequate' carer. A theoretical idealized view of care requires empathy and understanding plus skilled behaviour. In everyday language saying someone is a 'caring person' is merely to endorse them as a 'good person'.

The focus of the book is to capture this complexity through discussion of a number of perspectives. It attempts to summarize where we are now in our thinking on care and what has shaped our current position. Several chapters chart the evolution of the debate and the battles in the evolution of care as a recognized area of legitimate activity, with value and worth. The book also discusses the current controversies. An evidence-based approach is taken throughout the book, drawing on empirical research, practice wisdom and knowledge. Several principles and arguments underpin this book.

1   A lifecourse perspective is adopted throughout the book. Caregiving and receiving occurs across the lifecourse and not only at certain stages of it. Caregiving and receiving may be sequential or concurrent across the lifecourse; a carer one day may be a care recipient the next. Care may also be reciprocal and interdependent rather than one way. Assumptions of dependency may mask more complex notions of interdependence: for example, children contribute to family life offering parents emotional support; young carers offer support to disabled parents, while parents provide emotional and financial support. The care parents give to their children may later be reciprocated when the children care for their parents in their old age. An intergenerational perspective will also be emphasized.

Different discourses however dominate care at either end of the lifecourse (for example, prevention is an area of care in adult services whereas protection has become a primary concern in the children's arena of care). The framework of care also differs: for children the primary location of care is mainly within the parental household; for older people it may be in a different household. Funding structures for care are also different, reflecting the policy contexts in which care operates at different points in life, care of children being allied with education while adult care remains within a health framework. More often than not children are 'looked after' or in care of the local authority because of poverty and disadvantage; for adults care is experienced across social groups (Waine et al., 2005).

2   The recognition of care as a changing social construction. The basic premise for this draws on phenomenological philosophy stating that everyday life is multiple, fluid and based on interaction. 'Society . . . is a symbolic construct composed of ideas, meanings and language which is all the time changing through human action and imposing constraints and possibilities on human actors themselves' (Parton, 2003, p. 5). In developing a constructivist concept of care we have to develop a critical stance towards the 'taken for granted', accept numerous forms of knowledge, recognize that relationships are at the

heart of the approach and embrace reflexivity (Taylor and White, 2000), that is direct feedback from knowledge to action (Giddens, 1990). All these highlight issues and questions for the way we think about care. An example where care is socially constructed is through policy, with privatization and regulation of care in the forefront of policy development since 1990, when the nature of care and obligations around the provision of care changed. This is developed further in chapter 3.

As in every discussion of this kind, the terminology has evolved to reflect societal change in relation to the subject discussed. Care is no different. The language of care has changed and evolved from one where dependency was stressed to a rights base and empowerment perspective. The relationship between carer and person cared for was seen as one-way and one of dependency; over the last decade, mainly due to the disability movement, care has moved towards a rights-based framework. The language used in this book reflects such changes: caregivers are referred to as carers; care recipients as those who receive care.

A critical perspective on care will be adopted. This perspective challenges conventional approaches to carers and the notion of care, reframing care as an interdependent and connected concept – one which coexists with numerous other roles in an individual's life.

Our images of care are also shaped through our personal experiences, literature, art, photography (Bytheway and Johnson, 2005) and the media. Often stereotyped versions of care are portrayed, for example older people being depicted as frail and helped by younger people. Individual and societal understandings of care will consequently vary.

3   There are multiple perspectives on the concept of care; these are discussed throughout the book. Health and social care are not the sole arenas where care is played out, although they predominantly influence the thinking in this book. Even within health and social care there are different paradigms for understanding care, for example in how health care is organized in relation to social care. The book takes a wide and whole-system approach to care where appropriate, and the concept is discussed in its broadest sense, for example in the debates around productivity of carers who juggle work and care, addressed through workplace-based literature. Different disciplines (social

policy, nursing) and groups (disabled people, feminists) also contribute to the multiple perspectives and views on care.

Similarly multiple perspectives emerge from different models of care. An ecological model of care is emerging recognizing the importance of the broader environmental context of care. Both feminist and political 'ethics of care' have taken on prominence in the last decade in shaping the concept of care, and debates on rights, citizenship, risks and justice have all influenced how care is defined and assessed.

4   The concept of care is shaped by our cultural values and the book aims to take a cross-cultural, cross-national approach drawing on how care is experienced in different cultural and national settings. Most of the debates surrounding care have been in developed Western societies and therefore the concept of care is primarily discussed throughout from a white ethnocentric perspective. This is not to devalue other ideas of care promoted by non-Western societies. The care debates in Europe have focused on the individual, the family, and society in general, yet care is a notion that also needs to be debated at tribal and local community levels. On an international level the Universal Declaration of Human Rights sets out the framework in which care should be viewed.

5   Care also has a history as well as a geography, and as a concept changes in time and space. The care received by mentally ill patients in the early twentieth century, for example, would be reframed today as one of cruelty (see chapter 9). Care viewed over a lifetime will be different if it is episodic or continuous or if it involves intense periods of time. Care received in later life may also relate back to care given to children, as abusive parents may be abused themselves later in life. The concept of care itself has a long and contested history.

6   The importance of 'lived experiences' is echoed by Gubrium (1995) and the voices of 'care' are represented in the book from a number of studies of carers, care recipients and professionals. The book draws on the voices of those experiencing care as well as those who practise care in a number of settings.

7   A personal and professional journey of care. My ideas represented in the book have also been shaped by personal and professional experience as a long-distance carer of older parents

and a professional social worker. My particular interest in care as a subject arose out of working as a naïve care assistant at an older people's home in the 1970s: a concern for frail and sick residents and the experience of participating in a public sector organization led me to undertake social work studies and to become a community social worker with older people. The concept (duty) of care pervaded my remit. This book has come about following such a long-standing interest in understanding the complexities of assessing the need for and providing care.

It has also evolved from personal experiences of providing emotional and occasional practical care to my parents at a distance. What I have attempted in the book is to marry the personal and professional and to wrestle with the dilemmas that both create.

The structure of the book

The book will be organized around key issues and debates in policy, practice and theory. The aim of this book will be to highlight the current controversial debates centred on the concept of care, charting the issues as they apply to childhood and adolescence as well as midlife and old age. There is no one simplified argument running through the book; if there is continuity then it is around the complexity and multidimensionality of care. The book will take a broad multidimensional approach, although the main concentration will be on health and social care focusing on older people, adults with disabilities, people with mental health problems and people with a learning disability. Debates at the macro level of policy and practice as well as at the micro level will be considered.

Each chapter will start by providing the context for the arguments in the chapter. In addition each chapter will map the evolution and history of the debate and readers will be guided to the influential texts on the debates, drawing on 'classic studies' and research which had great influence on the issues (for example, Janet Finch and Dulcie Groves' *A Labour of Love*, 1983, advancing the feminist debate on caring). Every chapter will review and critique existing research and thinking in order to examine the ways in which different perspectives have influenced our understanding of care. Empirical research will be used to illustrate the debates. Each chapter will include theory, research, and practice. The book relates theory to practice by drawing on examples from social work, nursing and social care settings to illustrate the main concepts. Different practice scenarios are woven through each chapter.

Chapter 2 introduces the concept of care in its broadest sense, asking: How do we define care? What is its purpose? What are the boundaries of care? To set the context for the book as a whole, the main arguments in the book and current debates surrounding the concept of care will be presented, examining the nature of existing research and discourses in this area. Changing meanings, broadening definitions and the reconceptualizing of care, from a needs and dependency framework to a rights perspective and from an institutional to community location, will be explored. Theoretical developments, for example the ethics of care, will be charted. The complexity and multidimensionality of the concept of care is illustrated in this chapter.

Chapter 3 will address the social policy of care. Who provides and pays for care, whether it is the state, family, voluntary, independent or private sector, has been an increasingly important area for debate. The shifting balance of care between formal and informal, public and private sectors will be explored. The demographics of care, setting the structural potential for the need and provision of care, will be briefly examined along with the other drivers for change in social policy approaches to care. The social policy debates around care have a long history and the historical context will be addressed through three areas: the provision of care (looking at the move from institutional to community care, from public to private provision of care, from formal to informal, with a final section addressing the integration of health and social care); the payment for care (with the long-term care debate, debates on modernizing services around the preventative agenda, and the costs for carers); and the social construction of care, which is illustrated throughout the chapter.

The escalating costs of care have been tied in with arguments and myths concerning a demographic time bomb. There has been a major public debate about long-term care and how best to fund it since the 1930s. Long-term care insurance and developing alternative arrangements and models of care have been considered as part of the solution. Funding also raises complex theoretical issues, such as what can be demanded from the state, and chapter 3 will also debate the rights and responsibilities tied into funding care. The debates around targeting care will be highlighted. The economics of care can be in harmony with good practice (as in the case of the move from institutional to community care), yet this is not always the case and the rationing of resources may clash with professional notions of what constitutes good practice. Withdrawing personal care from older people because of the local council's restrictive criteria may mean a lack of care or reliance on inferior provision. It may also result in reliance on family care alone.

As new forms and patterns of care emerge involving friends, neighbours and other kin, the question of whether 'the family' is the primary location for care is again raised. Chapter 4 addresses the question: Is the family still primary in the care relationship? To what extent do others outside the family network provide care and how are these relationships negotiated? The chapter starts by examining the changing dynamics of family life, with the growth of divorce, reconstituted families and different living arrangements, as well as attitudes and aspirations within families. The impact of such changes on a commitment to care is discussed drawing on the work of Williams and her colleagues (2004), who argue that despite change families remain resilient and 'operate on the basis of "doing the right thing"'. The ethic of care is introduced in this chapter.

Why do people care? The debate on obligation and duty will draw on the seminal work of Janet Finch and Jennifer Mason in *Negotiating Family Responsibilities* (1993) and trace the developments over the last two decades. The impact of care on relationships has been dominated by research on stress and burden. Increasingly the debate on care relationships is turning its attention to looking at the satisfactions and positives of caregiving and receiving and the reciprocity and interdependence within relationships. New areas of research have also emerged in the last decade highlighting the care needs of different people in the family. Carers in employment, for example, have surfaced on the agendas of employers and trade unions, casting a different light on the issues and conceptualization of care. Research on young carers and on older people with learning disabilities as well as carers juggling work and family life will be drawn on to illustrate these arguments. The chapter introduces recent work on care networks and looks at who else in the network provides care. By not assuming the family are central in the care relationship, network methodology enables us to look at wider significant relationships. Friends are found to be sources of help and support to adults.

Chapter 5 looks at the changing gendered notions of care and asks whether caring is still a feminist debate. Care first appeared on the policy agenda through the work of feminist writers and activists. Care was viewed centrally as a women's issue. However, increasing numbers of men are taking on the role of caregiver for children and adults. It has been argued that seeing care as a women's issue reinforces the gendered low-status nature of care in terms of both informal care and formal paid carework.

This chapter will trace the feminist and disability perspectives and evaluate their impact on our current understanding of care. There is ample evidence to assert that the early feminists made a considerable impact by exposing the stresses of carers in caring for older people and the difficulties mothers faced in their pursuit of equality with men in the workplace. However, users and particularly disabled people were critical of an approach that viewed them as dependent on their carers. To address the equality debate the concept of care was debated on the basis of rights and citizenship. More recently this approach has been challenged and an 'ethic of care' perspective advocated. The chapter looks at the utility of this approach and the benefits it can bring to promoting the value of care at both individual and societal levels.

Chapter 6 draws on cross-cultural issues and the ethnicity of care. Most of the literature on carers presents ethnocentric views of care and Western perspectives of carers. There is an increasing need to develop cross-cultural views of care and to question whether care can be ethnically and culturally sensitive. In the UK increasing numbers of children from ethnic minorities are disproportionately entering the care system, while at the opposite end of the age range few older people from minority groups have their needs met in the formal care arena. The chapter studies the UK situation in terms of the literature on its response to care needs of minority ethnic groups. Part of the system's failure to meet those care needs is that it addresses issues purely from the basis of race and ethnicity. The chapter outlines the arguments around multiculturalism.

Chapter 7 explores the geography of care: Where is the best location for care? An age-old debate has focused on the ideal location for care, residential- or community-based. Classic studies such as *Asylums* by Erving Goffman (1961) and *The Last Refuge* by Peter Townsend (1962) will be drawn on to highlight issues of the debate such as stigma, institutionalization and quality of care. Such studies (along with funding concerns) influenced the policy steer to placing importance on the notion of independence, family and community care. In the child care arena similar concerns were voiced over residential care for 'looked after' children with evidence continuing to support kinship care, foster care and adoption over residential provision.

The chapter however will focus on, examine and evaluate locations of care at stages of the lifecourse other than childhood. It will look at emerging issues such as distance and migration in relation to care seeking. The debate is increasingly being focused on the globalization of care and the distances people travel to negotiate care and to act as caregivers. This has a considerable impact on people juggling work and family life, and the impact of care on work will be discussed. In concluding this chapter a 'caringscapes' approach connecting the social and the spatial is advocated in taking the argument forward.

The professionalization of care is addressed in chapter 8. The debates that have been raging include a discussion of the boundaries of care and paradigms under which care operates and is practised; interdisciplinary rivalry between health and social care; the debate on the changing context of social care and social work; the management of care; the low status of carework; and the role of the professional carer.

Relationships with the formal sector have also been challenged with the promotion of users' and carers' voices in the policy and practice debate, but whether the evolution of user groups has led to a change in the power dynamics within this relationship is debatable. Notions of empowerment, participation and autonomy and person-centred approaches will be discussed in this context.

The chapter concludes by looking at whether power relationships at the heart of a professionalized approach can be shifted by advocating a community-based social model of care incorporating an ethics of care.

The penultimate chapter looks at the opposite of our ideal vision of 'care' and examines neglect and abuse within the child care, mental health and residential care systems. Such scandals have led to the concept of care being redefined as risk aversion and protection. The conflicting demands that 'care and control' and 'support and surveillance' place upon carers and care and the risks that vulnerable people and their carers face will be highlighted. The debate concerning social justice in the care system will be explored within this context.

In the concluding chapter, the discussion will look at the debates that are likely to continue and at new debates likely to emerge. For example, with increasing emphasis on technology (medical, communications and monitoring technologies, for example) in the care arena, debate will centre on the appropriate use of technologies to promote care. Consideration will be given to how these debates impact on our future expectations of care. In so doing we will return to the demographic, social and economic aspects of care. Whether there will be a crisis in care is a debatable question which is raised in the chapter. Although the jury has yet to return a decision there are signs that a reconceptualization of care is long overdue. In advocating a new definition of care the chapter puts forward the main tenets that will underpin the argument: these consist of citizenship, an ethic of care and a social ecology model of care.

The book is intended to introduce students to the ideas surrounding care as a concept primarily within the health and social sciences. It does not provide an exhaustive synthesis of the issues but I hope will help unravel some of the complexity of the care debates, broaden perspectives on care and encourage further study. Care is a fluid concept and will continue to be shaped by our real experiences. For social workers, nurses and those engaged in social care and similar professions the book aims to deepen understanding of their professional and often personal experiences. It raises issues and dilemmas that will be familiar and enables them to explore and question their own practice assumptions, values and assessments. It encourages an examination of how practice and decision making may be influenced by these concepts. Appropriate practice scenarios throughout the book encourage readers to reflect on their practice and knowledge.

2
Definitions and Boundaries, Meanings and Identities

In this chapter I explore the diverse and contended definitions and meanings of care, investigate its purpose and attempt to examine its boundaries and contested areas. Definitions of care, however, have not remained static and the chapter charts the development of the concept of care both in relation to children and adults and in particular in relation to public policy. In conclusion the multidimensional aspects of care are summarized and emerging definitions of care as rights-based are presented and challenged. These debates are necessary if we are to arrive at a definition of 'good' and 'poor' care that can be applied universally.

What is care?

The word 'care' has many different meanings, dimensions and values attached to it. Whereas care in the late twentieth century was associated with the 'welfare' or 'support' of a person, or a 'liking of' or a 'responsibility to' a person, in the past it had more negative associations. In Anglo-Saxon the meaning of the word was sorrow, anxiety, burden or concern (Cameron and Moss, 2001, p. 4). Until recently care has been seen as an impediment to work, restricting women to the domesticity of home or, if they were performing 'care' in the workplace, to low-status, oppressive carework jobs. The recognition of emotional fulfilment and rewards for carers is now recasting this concept in a more positive light. A rights-based approach (see chapter 5) has also supported a more positive definition of care. There are many distinctions in the term 'care'. The verb caring 'for' can imply an action toward and a passive dependence of one person on another, and caring 'about' or 'taking care of' can mean caring in a more detached way, for example taking care of or caring about people with malaria. The care relationship in the former sense is often defined by dependency and can be viewed in a negative way. The debate on how to promote 'active ageing' takes a counter position; its supporters advocate breaking the link between care and dependency in an attempt to rid the concept of care of its negative associations.

The nouns 'caregiver' and 'care recipient' are also loaded with similar meanings of powerful and powerless. As Harrington Meyer, Herd and Michel (2000, p. 2) suggest, the word caregiver implied 'a free and willing service based on choice'. The literature also disaggregates different types of carers (by age, gender, sexual orientation, class and race) and types of care based on the nature (personal, financial, emotional) or care recipient (older person, person with a learning disability, with mental health problems). Care therefore involves tasks, roles and relationships. Care is also associated with privacy, emotion and need. It is a disposition as well as a practice (Tronto, 1993).

Care can also be seen as a process in its ongoing nature. In discussing this aspect Nolan, Grant and Keady (1996) point out that caring is often only thought about if it involves instrumental support, yet care begins much earlier through a process of anticipatory care moving to supervisory care. Others dispute this. According to Litwin and Auslander (1990) it is only when support is needed because of ill health or functional limitations that it can be termed care.

The process or transition into care can also involve locational change as the environment fails to meet the care needs of the person and a balance between the individual and their environment becomes more difficult to achieve. Older people will cope with such changes depending on their personal competence and ability to adapt themselves or the environment, which may be oppressive. Adjustment and adaptation to place changes are also important to preserve self-identity (Lawton and Nahemow, 1973). Tronto (1993), however, extends our understanding of care. She defines care as implying 'a reaching out to something other than self: it is neither self-referring nor self-absorbing. Second, care implicitly suggests that it will lead to some type of action' (p. 102). She goes on to broaden the traditional notion of care from a dyadic or individualistic position (a relationship between two people) to caring for objects such as the environment (Fisher and Tronto, 1990). Care is part of the fabric of society and is integral to social development (p. 33). The complexity of definition is echoed through Finch and Groves's 1983 book *A Labour of Love*.

Definitions of care are not straightforward and have proved contentious. One reason is that the borders surrounding our concept of care are neither clear nor settled. Moreover, the boundaries, for example between care and education for children and between care, housing and health for adults, are moving and becoming less distinct. In a policy context care and welfare are synonymous and can span health and social arenas. Care is also played out in the formal (for example, professional) and informal (for example, family) arena, with different values and status attached to each domain, despite similar tasks and roles being performed in each.

Consequently, it is difficult to set boundaries to care. Care can also be seen as a holistic notion pervading all human relationships and activity. It is a central part of life, binding together families, friends and communities. It is embedded in social relations. Brannen and Heptinstall (2003) describe it as 'the engine of family life' and Kitwood (1997, p. 128) acknowledges 'to have concern for another person is above all else, to experience a feeling, a movement of the soul, in which that person's being is honoured and respected as if it were one's own'. Care therefore also incorporates love, solidarity, exchange, altruism and spirituality.

These notions have been embodied in the principles of society through obligation, duty, love and loyalty. Emotion and guilt have been strong features underlying affective ties concerned with the giving and receiving of care. It is also seen as an attitude, disposition and orientation (Tronto, 1993).

In relation to professional settings it is important to remember that care is a 'normal' part of everyday life through the lifecourse and not to pathologize those in need of care; on the other hand it is important not to assume care as 'natural' for certain individuals such as daughters.

Case study

Janice cares for her parents Ruby and Jack, who are in their 90s. They live together in a mid-terraced house in the centre of a large city. Ruby suffered a stroke six years ago and Jack is in the early stages of Alzheimer's disease. One may assume that Janice is the primary carer; yet a closer look at the situation reveals that Janice is severely disabled and uses a wheelchair following a car accident several years ago. She relies on care workers for short periods each day to help her with personal tasks and to take care of all practicalities such as shopping and food preparation for her parents. Despite 'outside' help, Janice views herself as a carer, providing care as part of a lifetime of love and concern reciprocated over her lifetime. Ruby also sees herself as a pivotal carer for the family. Ruby doesn't see Janice as a carer but a daughter – a tension of positioning within the family, highlighted when Janice applied for a carer's allowance.

This practice example highlights the need to carefully assess the whole situation and circumstances before making assumptions about who cares for whom, the strengths and weaknesses of different members, and the interdependencies and reciprocity that occur within the family, not just in the assessment visit but across the lifecourse of the family. A further issue for social workers in this context may be one of where to concentrate limited resources; without external assistance from care workers the home situation would not be sustainable.

Care is often associated with warm, positive, meaningful relationships. However, the act of caring can also engender feelings of ambivalence and conflict as hinted above in the practice example. Caregiver and care recipient needs may be different. A new dimension introduced here is that of ambivalence. Ambivalence is likely to be found increasingly in intergenerational relations as complexity and diversity characterize family relations and lifestyles (Coontz, 2000). There is a growing sense that contemporary society is characterized by rapid social change and uncertainties over the nature of social relationships. Individuals are unsure about the roles they have in family life, perhaps especially those which relate to care relationships. These uncertainties threaten previously held norms about family relationships and mutual obligations and lead to opposing and conflicting emotions within the family.

Despite permeating all human relationships care is culturally specific. What constitutes good quality care will also be culturally defined. We cannot assume that our ways of knowing and understanding are the same as those of others. There is no 'truth' about care or any objective universal definition of care. This calls for us to take a critical stance in the way we see the world. Knowledge and actions are interrelated (Parton, 2003) and our understandings are based on the relationships we engage in. Care, as we outlined in chapter 1, is a social construction. The specificity of care however should not impede our view of the wider global dimensions. Despite its cultural definition there is universal difficulty in raising the concept of care to its proper status (Tronto, 1993).

The dichotomization of the 'carer' and 'cared for' also promotes a notion of the lack of agency. The notion of dependency (particularly if it is socially constructed) deprives the older person of agency within the relationship. For older people who are carers, both carer and cared for will have similar needs, and the carer's health and social care needs may be only marginally different from those of the older person for whom they care, for example, between Janice and Ruby or Ruby and Jack above. Interdependency and help are more relevant terms in this context (Shakespeare, 2000) although neither term engages with the problem of inequality and lack of personal capacity.

Fine and Glendinning (2005) develop a new understanding of the social contexts of this dichotomy of care and dependency which has arisen from different theoretical paradigms. They argue that it is important to recognize the contested positions of such terms and to 'rehabilitate the meanings inherent in the terms' (p. 612). The power differential is a crucial element in any re-analysis. Kittay (1999) argues for a notion of 'nested dependencies' as a fundamental part of the lifecourse. We cannot be autonomous throughout our lives and will rely on help from childhood onward. Inequalities of power will be prevalent in dependency relationships but this may not just be one way. Older people in receipt of direct payments for example may have the power to hire and fire formal carers. Economic, physical and sexual abuse of carers is also not unheard of. 'Nested dependencies . . . link those who need support with those who help them and which in turn link the helpers to a set of broader supports' (p. 615). Kittay sees dependency as an effective conceptual tool for examining the relationship between those who require assistance and those who provide it. Viewing these concepts with a more positive emphasis echoes the writings of Tronto (1993).

Care can be defined through its complexity. It is complex because it involves all aspects of life. On the other hand care is defined as a distinct policy. Graham summed up the complexity in 1983 as follows: 'caring defines a specific type of social relationship based upon both affection and service, and, moreover, [. . .] these two interlocking transactions have been carefully dismantled by social scientists, and reconstructed within the separate disciplinary domains of psychology and social policy. In this process of reconstruction, the everyday experience of caring as a labour of love has been lost' (p. 28).

The purpose of care

The purpose is often defined by the reason why care is needed. If you are receiving medical care the need for care arises because of ill health or an accident; if you receive social care it may be because you are unable to perform the activities of daily living. Care can be an end in itself – care as an expression of who a person is or what a society values can demonstrate this.

In *Community Care* (1997) Williams argues that the right to choose when to be cared for matters more than the purpose of care. Care can be provided in a relationship that is interdependent so it is not only the person cared for but also the carer who can benefit from being in a care role. Who is it for as well as why, are questions to be asked.

Some aspects of care are enshrined in legislation. In relation to children, care is a statutory duty, and failing to care for, or neglecting, a child can lead to a removal of the child from the family (Howe, 2005). Parents have a legal responsibility to care for their children but there are no fixed rules of obligation (Brannen and Moss, 2003).

Care in the context of health and social care is about maintenance, not about changing people. It involves giving the understanding and practical help required to maintain the status quo in people's circumstances. In policy terms, social care has been about achieving maximum independence, (re)acquiring basic living skills and, at its most ambitious, achieving full potential (Department of Heath, 1989, para 1.8). Keeping or maintaining people who are chronically ill or disabled at home as independent for as long as possible with dignity has become a specific purpose of care policy in the UK (Welsh Assembly Government, 2006).

Two contrasting philosophies of care have emerged which reflect on the one hand a maintenance approach (or, as some term it, compensatory care) and on the other a therapeutic philosophy of care. In relation to the former, often nothing is provided, whereas in the latter, intensive forms of intervention may prevail. Age may play a part in this, in relation to ethical decision making at the end of life for example. Therapeutic intervention may not be seen to be justified or effective.

A further purpose in care is that of 'servicing' (Land, 1991). This can be described as 'being there to wait, to listen, to respond and to attend the needs and desires of others; to worry when difficulties are anticipated, to deal with one's sense of guilt when problems are not successfully resolved' (Balbo, 1987).

In a policy context the realm of care provision was until the early 1980s firmly rooted in the public sector. However care is increasingly commodified and has entered the market place as a business. The purposes of care therefore allow and meet the needs of a different and diverse set of actors. Care can be broken into different tasks and set time periods which can be costed and therefore can be traded. The boom in private residential care provision in the UK in the 1980s demonstrated the nature of supply and demand in care (see chapter 3). The provision of residential care increased enormously as public funds became available to expand this sector and later decreased enormously in response to the lack of public funding or social insurances to pay for such provision. Care as a business has become important in a number of EU member states such as the Netherlands, the UK, Belgium, Germany and France (Cameron and Moss, 2001). The emotional aspects however cannot be costed or detailed in a contract and this has led to the devaluing of care and underestimation of its complexity. Carework takes place within an economic exchange and so care is viewed as a product (Stone, 2000a).

Returning to our care scenario, the local care agency provides thirty minutes of care several times a day to Ruby, Jack and Janice. Yet despite this being a long-standing arrangement there is frustration that often there are different people coming into the house every few weeks making it difficult to build up a relationship of trust, or even to catch up on local news. The emotional side of caring is often neglected by agencies in their allocation of time.

Care may also serve educational purposes. In Europe a pedagogical approach is adopted. Care in Denmark and Sweden, for example, is closely linked with tasks supporting education and development. Although this has developed in relation to children the concept of pedagogy is creeping into the care arena of older adults.

Caring may also be tied up with identity, particularly for women who are socialized into servicing or nurturing roles. The relinquishing of their carer role may mean a loss of identity (Barnes, 1997) and in some cases caring in a private familial setting is replaced by taking on employment in a public care setting such as residential care or home care.

Brechin (1998) argues that the approach to care may be to look at what constitutes 'good' or 'poor' care based on the purpose of care rather than focusing on the definition itself. Taking the agreed aim of 'promoting autonomy in the context of supported living' (p. 175) as a measure of 'good' care she draws up a model of care where an evaluation of the quality of care centres on three areas:

- the measure to which the care relationship enhanced or limited the options available to promote choice and opportunity
- the interpersonal processes in the relationship
- the intrapersonal experience, and the impact of the care relationship on self-esteem.

Defining the domain and drawing boundaries

Care can also be seen as a contentious issue with a number of heated debates surrounding it. Some of these debates run throughout the book. As Daly and Lewis (2000) note, 'care lies at the interstices on many of the most interesting dichotomies at the heart of social provision' (p. 282).

One of the major distinctions is whether care is formal or informal, paid or unpaid. Formal care is seen to be paid, and formally organized, regulated and monitored, while informal care is unpaid and something associated with family care, carried out in the home, usually unregulated and unmonitored. There are however a number of similarities binding the two domains. The similarities between paid and unpaid work are associated with a number of factors: women employ women as the primary carers; the meaning of work and acknowledgement that the emotional side (termed 'emotional labour' by Hochschild, 1983) provides the satisfaction with work can be found in both areas; the tasks in formal and informal care are often intimate, for example, involving bodywork which can be seen as 'dirty work' and low status (Twigg, 2001); many jobs in the formal sector are regarded as unskilled; in informal care all work is seen as unskilled; and additionally in both there are major issues about availability and quality. For both formal but, more so, informal care the work is hidden and silent. Consequently it is not often a subject for significant public debate. It has been the association between the two arenas that has led some commentators to conclude that the low status of carework is because of its link to domesticity and women's work.

There is debate around the word 'informal' itself, which can be offensive to those carers and care recipients who plan and organize their care routines and patterns; there is nothing necessarily informal about many of these arrangements. In our case study Janice, Ruby and Jack have a routinized day due to the necessity for coordination between homecare workers, Jack's day care and personal routines for Janice and Ruby. The pattern of care cannot be described as informal, and without structure to the day it would be difficult for the family to function.

Further debates centre on the notion of 'best' care and whether paying for care locks a service user into a contractual position where 'best' care can be provided and regulated by rules and through standards. The question here is whether rules ensure better care than the basis of a relationship alone, which could be less secure and binding. Paid versus unpaid is a debate framed under individualized (person-centred) or standardized care (see chapter 8 for a critique of this). The introduction of direct payments has challenged the notion of who defines best care with service users now having the choice of who to employ, rather than the decision being left to a professional.

One of the more recent debates on the boundary has been the distinction between professional and unprofessional. This debate has been heightened in relation to the distinction between social care and social work. Increasingly social work has been described within a social care framework. 'Social care non cash services are provided by social workers and other professional groups for user groups such as children and families, older people and people with disabilities' (Munday, 1998, p. 4).

Increasingly however the link between social care and social work lies within the value base rather than the provision of care. Davies and Connolly (1995) argue that carework, for example in residential care, follows similar principles and holds similar values to social work, including respect for the young person, promoting individual uniqueness, non-paternalism, self-actualization and freedom. Yet there are different components to social work. Social work with adults has been transformed into care management. The professional role is seen as navigating through the care system rather than providing the relational aspects of care. The emphasis, although placed on a needs-led approach to care, has in practical terms forced a service-led development, fitting people into existing services. Social workers in the early part of the twenty-first century providing assessment and gatekeeping are only offering limited care themselves.

The term 'social care' is a relatively recent one. One of the advantages of badging care as social care is that 'it transcends the conceptual dichotomies between the public and the private, the professional and the non-professional, the paid and the unpaid' (Kröger, 2001, p. 4). It also links child and adult care. The transcendent perspective of social care means that carework is understood as a similar practice wherever it is done (in or out of the home) and whoever it is done by (unpaid or paid workers). This does not mean that the provision of social care is straightforward and simple. Baldock and Ely (1996) refer to the 'paradox of complex mundaneity' (p. 203), the inherent complexity of everyday life with social care, characterized by cultural difficulties between public and private life, organizational problems as care needs are unpredictable, and economic complexities as financing varies from case to case.

One of the most contested debates surrounding care is where medical care stops and social care begins. The medical-social boundary has become a policy nightmare and this will be further discussed in relation to the professionalization of care in chapter 8. One of the areas of this debate has been funding for long-term and continuing care. Although this may be clear at institutional level, when it comes to the personal care for the individual what constitutes medical and social is difficult to define.

A key policy debate is tied to the shifting definitions of who needs care. In this context care is a social construct, and depends on eligibility assessed on certain criteria. Over the last decade the definition of need has narrowed to those most vulnerable and 'at risk'. What this constitutes is a focusing of care on certain sections of the population. The opposite would be a preventative agenda which would broaden the definition of a 'need' for care. Expectations of who we should care for and how we should care are again socially constructed. For example, with women returning to work care need has shifted – in relation to children, childcare has moved to become widespread and outside the home.

Further questions about the boundaries of care are seen in the debates surrounding care and support. When does support become care? Canadian work in this area shows that support networks do not necessarily become care networks (Keating et al., 2003). Care has traditionally focused on a dyadic relationship; care networks focus on a wider set of relationships.

Rights and choices play a key role in care. When and how care is provided is not straightforward. Who is responsible for deciding when help is to be offered and what type of help is necessary and when people have the right to be left alone are professional debates of considerable controversy. Some of these decisions are governed by legislation: for example when a person is defined as 'being at risk to self and other' through a mental disorder, care can be a compulsory admission to a psychiatric hospital by invoking the Mental Health Act 1983. Tied to the notion of rights however are risks and responsibilities. The right to care comes with the risk that poor quality care will be provided. Daly (2001) argues that the right to care is meaningless unless there is 'good quality care'. What constitutes 'good' or 'good enough' is a debatable issue.

Considering the above mental health example there is a question of whether care is about support or control. Care may have a control element. Linked to this is the question of who holds the power in the care relationship. There is a notion of dependency inherent in the way care relationships are conceived by society and in the location of care. Tronto argues that 'care delineates positions of power and power-lessness' (p. 122); 'us and them' (Morris, 1997) or 'others' (Tronto, 1993). In her view, that 'others' matter is the most difficult moral quality to establish in practice (p. 130). Paternalism can also result from power imbalances. Professionals involved in the family situation of Janice, Ruby and Jack feel the family is 'at risk'. The fragile system of care arrangements relies on good coordination, relationships and the empowerment of family members in their respective roles, yet this may be threatened by the power of their new GP, looking afresh at the situation, worried about the vulnerability within the family and suggesting that Ruby and Jack would be better off in residential care.

Care in an unfamiliar hospital setting with professionals controlling the environment can be disempowering. Age can play a part here. As we move through the lifecourse the nature of care shifts, from the relatively powerless position of babies to that of an equal, to being cared for by, or providing care to, friends and family. Children are however not altogether powerless. Reciprocity and interdependence are often undervalued in debates on care. However, even if there is reciprocity over the lifecourse, at any one time one person is likely to be in need of care from the 'other'. Interdependence, whether between members of a family or community, is illustrated in figure 2.1.

There are numerous other characteristics in the literature on care. There is a further distinction highlighted in policy between care for children and older people. Although social care may bind them together in policy terms, they have developed along separate paths; children are often referred to as 'looked after' in the care system; the same does not apply to adults. There are also notions of care in the criminal justice system raising the debate over justice and care. A more recent notion is of restorative justice, emphasizing care for the victim and the community focus of care. Rights, citizenship and justice are all encompassed in the notion of 'care' in this context.

In all these debates one of the key shifts is to blur the boundaries of care and not to make false dichotomies if care is to be valued. By blurring the boundaries we gain a new perspective on care at the margins and the intersections between private and public, professional and personal, and paid and unpaid. This is further discussed in subsequent chapters.

Figure 2.1

Development of the concept of 'care'

There are a number of distinct influences on the development of the concept of care, notably starting with the feminist movement in the 1960s. The gendered nature of 'caring' for women by women in both public and private spheres received both empirical and theoretical attention from feminist researchers over a sustained period of time. Major contributors to this debate were recognized in Janet Finch and Dulcie Groves's edited collection, *A Labour of Love* (1983). Within this gendered paradigm were a number of debates, for example whether a gender-neutral approach could be followed. A full discussion of this paradigm can be found in chapter 5 of this book. There were a number of critiques of this pervading paradigm. Although we are forty years on from the beginnings of the argument on care, feminist theory has developed very little, with the emphasis being on a critique of community care policies. The early writers focused the debate on gender alone and did not take into account age, sexual orientation or disability. They had very little to say about the diversity of carers' experiences, concentrating exclusively on the organization and experiences of white, non-disabled, heterosexual carers. Consequently they stereotyped situations in which carers found themselves, that is out of the labour market, independent rather than interdependent and in a reciprocal relationship, and providing care in the domestic 'home' setting. The multiple and often conflicting identities of women were ignored (hooks, 1981).

One of the main objections to the way in which care was framed was that it cast care recipients as dependent, passive and inert relative to caregivers. This, in more recent times, has led Williams (2001) to describe the care debate as moving in two different directions with an emphasis firstly on 'a paradigm of difference and diversity' (p. 207) which came from people who were marginalized in care policies. This was led by the disability movement with some arguing for a different language, such as 'support,' 'help' or 'personal assistance', to replace 'care' (Finkelstein, 1998; Morris, 1991; Oliver, 1990; Shakespeare, 2000; Clark, Dyer and Horwood, 1998). Help is what friends do and the friendship paradigm may be a more equitable term as it is based on altruism and voluntarism, unlike care which is often imposed through family relationships. They also argued that the power differential between providers and recipients of services should be challenged as this enforced dependency and patronized disabled people. The care notion placed disabled people into a dependency relationship with negative powerless implications for them as individuals. It cast them as burdens denying carers the freedoms to engage in paid work and have a life of their own. They argued that independence rather than interdependence should be stressed.

The social model advocated by the disability movement was articulated and developed by Campbell and Oliver (1996) and Oliver (2004) and was in contrast to the medical model. Its premise is based on a disablist society – environmental, economic and cultural barriers in society are encountered by people who are viewed by others as having some form of impairment. It has subsequently been widely accepted and developed by other groups, particularly those in learning disability and mental health (Beresford, 2004). The ecological model of care has been more prominent in relation to children and this is discussed in chapter 8.

There have been a number of critiques of the social model from disabled people themselves (Bury, 2000) for its lack of accommodation of impairment.

In a more recent article criticizing the notion of 'independent living', Oldman (2003) highlights the fact that social policy is based on this mantra, allowing governments to justify cutbacks in care provision. Linking care with independent living is itself criticized as patronizing, the term 'help', which conjures up a more equal relationship, being preferred.

The second direction of a 'universalist paradigm' and more recent debate has focused on the concept of citizenship, rather than gender alone. This notion has become synonymous with the emphasis on social rights. Rights, Sevenhuijsen (1998) argues, need to be claimed in relation to their connectedness to others – through their right *for* care and *to* care. This places the notion of care as a pervasive human condition with interdependent and lifecourse aspects. It is on the basis of this that policy is made in relation to both children and adults, with the rights of the child being enshrined in the UN Convention on the Rights of the Child and for adults in the Declaration of Human Rights. There are a number of critiques of this approach.

Jones and Wallace (1992) and Jones (2006) argue that childhood is often seen as static rather than a transition from dependency to independence. Policies are often not centred on interdependence and social rights of citizenship accrue to children through their parents or guardians. Access to rights is often withheld by parents so equity does not apply in the child care arena (Jones and Wallace, 1992) thus rendering some children vulnerable to abuse and neglect.

Ungerson (1987) also highlights the dilemmas in this approach to care: first, that carers are primarily located in the private world of the family and to impose authoritative rights in this setting is impossible. Secondly, whose rights take precedence? People in the caring relationship might well have conflicting needs and rights; taken to a societal level there will be problems matching differing needs and rights to services. To overcome these hurdles Ungerson talks about more general rights outside the caring relationship; this may help carers and recipients alike, for example through employment rights, rights to a basic income, etc.

Drewett (1999, p. 166) suggests there has been a lack of a theoretical base exploring the 'source and status' of rights, accompanied by a confusion between rights- and needs-based approaches. This becomes even more difficult when establishing legal rights to social care, where a definition of care, let alone an entitlement to rights, is far from clear. Who should define needs and rights also raises thorny issues for translating this issue into practice.

One of the most influential writers on this broader front is Tronto, who argues that care is a political, as well as moral, concept through which we can make judgements about the public world based on how well it cares. She developed the idea of care as a practice as well as a disposition. Tronto (1993) outlines four ethical elements in 'an ethic of care': attentiveness, responsibility, competence and responsiveness (p. 127), all of which need to be present and integrated if good care is required. 'That care givers value care is neither false consciousness nor romantic but a proper reflection of value in human life' (Tronto, p. 117).

Williams (2001) argues for a 'political ethics of care' to counteract the growing 'ethic of work' apparent in New Labour policies since 1997 such as the work–life balance campaign which helps carers into work. The debates around these issues are expanded in chapter 5.

What this section outlines is that the notion of care has developed from a perspective of dependency to a rights and citizenship debate, where it pervades all aspects of moral and political life. This moral or ethical dimension of care embraces a collective as much as an individual approach, introduces care as a form of social capital and allows a set of values to guide human agency (Sevenhuijsen, 2000). In the case example Janice should have full rights as a citizen – having a right to pursue employment, leisure, etc – and not be viewed as dependent in all areas of her life.

This chapter has demonstrated the complexity of the term 'care'. 'It is ambiguous and contested . . . used in such diverse ways that it is in danger of losing its core meaning' (Daly and Lewis, 2000, p. 284).

In conclusion, as Moss (2003) has outlined, the notion of care is 'multidimensional', encompassing caring about, which involves seeing and recognizing needs, understanding needs and selecting means and choosing various strategies for action; caring for, which involves taking responsibility for initiating caring activities, requiring empathy and judgement; caregiving, which involves concrete work; and care receiving, which includes the reactions of others to whom care is directed. In relation to our case study of Ruby, Jack and Janice, the social care agency may 'care about' their situation yet it is the social worker who may initiate care and care workers who may provide the practicalities of 'caring for' the family along with family members themselves.

Care is about tasks and labour, both physical and emotional. It is a practice involving certain ability factors: time, material resources, knowledge and skill, social relationships and feelings. Care also has to be discussed as an ethic attaching particular value to responsibility, responsiveness and integrity.

Care involves reciprocity and interdependency. It is part of a wider set of network relationships across the lifecourse: at some point, almost everyone will assume the role of receiver as well as provider of care. Providing good quality care involves 'emotional labour', the giving of self within social relations. As Moss (2003) argues, it is not just the emotion expressed between people but what goes on within people that affects caring. Caring also calls for multiple perspectives from different client or service user groups;

professional groups such as nursing and social work; feminists; disabled people; anti-racist commentators who may have concerns about the ethnocentralism of care; and social policy analysts concerned about costs and construction of community care packages.

3
The Social Policy of Care

On a micro, individual, level the concept of care is played out through intimate and professional relationships; on a macro level it is social policy that has shaped the concept. This chapter attempts to map out the social policy canvas on which the concept of care has evolved. In policy terms the concept has taken centre stage in debates about the future of welfare, partly driven by the demographics of care, the models of welfare and political ideology.

The literature on care is dominated by debates in policy. Whether we are discussing the boundaries between family and state or obligation linked to kinship and rights as citizens these are all constructed by social policy. Like the notion of care itself policy surrounding care is complex. 'To do justice to the complexity means that welfare states must adopt a multi-dimensional approach. The policy landscape surrounding care is therefore potentially very crowded' (Daly, 2001, p. 37).

Despite policy being a central area of care the opposite has not been the case: care has not been central to policy. Daly and Lewis (2000) argue that care can be a category which improves the depth and quality of welfare state analysis. Three dimensions of care – care as labour, care within a framework of obligations and responsibility, and care as an activity with costs – bring together care as activities and relations with the political, economic and social context to provide a basis for cross-national comparisons of the changing welfare regimes. The concept of care can be used analytically at both macro level (through the role of cash and services and the political activity of provision by and among the different sectors) and the micro level ('both through women's work and the individual's experience of welfare in society' (p. 286)).

Through this 'bridging of public and private' Daly and Lewis (2000) argue that 'the concept should serve as a useful category of analysis to uncover the nature and boundaries of welfare state provision and how they vary across time and national frontiers' (p. 287). Changes in welfare state activity have moved 'care' centre stage to any consideration of policy. Such changes have centred on shifts between the state, the family and the market as providers of care; the shift in relations between cash and services as the mode of provision; between the carer and the cared for as the recipient of that provision; shifting gender relations through the feminization of work and the diminishing role of the male breadwinner; and the changing demographics of young and old. Through a reconceptualization of care embedding it in the social and political economy, changes in welfare states can be mapped through the ways in which their 'welfare mix' is changing and the consequences for how care is delivered and by whom. The commodification of care across several countries in Europe, and particularly the UK for example, has led to targeting of services to those greatest in need with 'informal carers' supporting those who do not meet such criteria. 'Thus with the concept of care, the ethical issues that underlie contemporary welfare state restructuring are drawn to the centre of analysis' (p. 292).

Care has become the concern of policy across the board – health, social, employment, education, incomes policies and prison policy. Who provides care, whether it be the state, family, voluntary, independent or private sector, and the mixture and balance of such providers are increasingly important areas for debate. Over the last twenty years the equilibrium between sectors has shifted dramatically, altering the face of welfare and bringing the concept of care to the forefront of historic debate. The resulting fragmentation of care in policy and the plethora of systems have made this an area of complexity and controversy. In this chapter the shifting balance of care provision from institution to community, from formal to informal care, and from public to private sectors will be explored. The chapter illustrates some of these concepts by drawing on a case study of Jonathan, an older man with learning disabilities, who has witnessed changes in provision of care through his life.

The payment and costs of care are intricately tied to the provision of care. The dichotomy between informal care (apparently cost-free to the exchequer) and formal care (paid) is too simplistic, yet has formed the basis of numerous debates. One key debate is how to fund long-term care for older people. Similarly the fact that the NHS is free at the point of access whereas social care has to be paid for has led to debates on the fault line between health and social care. Additionally, this area of welfare has been limited by lack of public investment and financial cutbacks. Who provides care and what it costs have dominated but there has been less discussion of the concept of care itself. Shifting political ideologies and cultures have changed the notion of care and to some extent driven our understanding. Yet there is no clear view of what organizational structures and partnership arrangements meet different needs for care.

It is beyond the scope of this book to detail all the history and debates surrounding the development of care services for older people (Means, Richards and Smith, 2000) or for younger people (Hendrick, 1994). It is only in the last century that the notion of care has been expressed in legislation but the voice of children and adults has been missing. One of the trends until recently has been the low status with which older people (compared to children) have been viewed in policy terms. From the above it is evident that the moulding of 'care' in policy has been around different service user groups – older people, children, adults with a learning disability, with mental health needs or a physical disability – with their interests not being seen to overlap.

There are however a number of drivers to the social policy of care which have raised its profile in the welfare arena. These drivers have been aired in a number of debates centring on the development of the postmodern state questioning the balance between individuals, families, communities and the state in the provision and costs of care. Changes in the postmodern state raise fundamental questions about the definition of care, the micro experiences of care recipients and their families, and the macro responses of societies to their needs. The chapter considers such factors in relation to older adults.

The drivers of policy on care

The demographics of care

- Changes in family structure and roles, and greater geographical dispersion will mean that there may be less informal unpaid care.
- In addition to these factors, the number of over 85s will double between 2001 and 2041.

The UK has an ageing population due to a decline in fertility rates and the longevity of its population. This is accompanied by the demand for increasing numbers of women to enter the shrinking workforce. Consequently there is an increasing demand for care at both ends of the lifecourse – both for childcare to enable parents to return to work and to provide care to older frail people – but a decrease in supply as the availability of informal carers is reduced. Household structures are also changing with many people increasingly living in solo households as divorce and singlehood increases. The picture of younger and older generations living in close proximity and within households together providing reciprocated care can no longer be assumed. Increasing distance between families has several consequences for care as illustrated in chapter 7.

Morbidity and mortality

- Advances in treatment mean there are now people growing older with a long-term disability. This is particularly the case in relation to people with a learning disability. There are costs of meeting extra health and social care needs in the event of failing health.

• Carers themselves are also likely to be 'elderly'.

Increasing care needs will come with an ageing population. Although disability rates for older people have hardly changed since the 1980s, increasing longevity will see many healthy people in older age. However it also brings what can be termed 'the survival of the sickest'. People who would previously not have been able to survive into late old age can now do so due to treatment of previously fatal and chronic illnesses. People with a learning disability are also surviving longer. This will be gendered as women suffer from higher rates of morbidity than men. People will spend a longer period of their lifecourse either as carers or in receiving care.

Employment and workplace changes

Women's employment is growing in the UK, especially among women with children. This means a shortage of informal carers for children and adults requiring care. Mooney and Statham (2002), in their research on transitions after 50, found that grandparents were also engaged in employment rather than providing a source of informal support to children and grandchildren. The increasing insecurity of pension provision and rising household debt puts pressure on this generation to remain in work rather than retire.

With people having children later in life couples are also likely to have children and ageing parents requiring care at the same time. The 'sandwich generation' (Brody, 1981) is likely to rise, yet these are the same people required in the workplace.

Attitudinal changes

• Changes in labour costs – especially if there is a shortage of people prepared to work in care services.

There have been shifts in attitudes particularly in relation to women returning to work. The traditional household of male breadwinner is no longer an expectation in the twenty-first century and dual earner households have become a necessity rather than a luxury. Men are also encouraged to take parental leave and to switch roles although the evidence so far is not encouraging on this as a trend.

Attitudes also differ in terms of how families organize their care arrangements, with some families wanting to take care of their own children rather than have others care for them. The stigmatization of care in certain areas such as mental health or childcare has also resulted in policy shifts leading to blurring the boundaries between care, education and play, for example, by removing care of children from a social services function to one of education (Moss, 2003).

Workplace attitudes are also shifting with parental leave being accommodated, yet there is still a long way to go for employers to recognize the needs of those working carers who have elder care responsibilities.

Values and norms in care

• There are greater expectations and demands from the public in the way long-term care is delivered.

Given the above social changes, the central policy debates have revolved around two major areas: who provides care and how it can be financed. The remainder of this chapter addresses the variety of debates under these headings looking at changes in provision, and the costs of care and its financing.

The provision of care

Debates on the scope of care: long-term care and home care

The policy around the provision of 'care' is tied into the development of the concept of community care. There are debates on the nature of community and reality of community care, for example whether it is attainable to have true communities caring for each other or whether in practice care can only be provided at an individualistic and familial level, rather than at community level. Yet the notion of locating care outside of institutions has driven policy for over fifty years. One of the enduring questions has been whether good quality care is best provided in institutions or in the community (see chapter 7). Despite clear evidence of the failures of residential care (Townsend, 1962; Miller and Gwynne, 1972; Goffman, 1961), the jury on this was out for some time. The verdict in favour of community care surfaced in policy during the 1970s and only became reality with the 1990 NHS and Community Care Act. Ironically the New Right policies led to a growth in residential care in the 1980s, contrary to the stated policy of home care. Throughout much of the twentieth century reliance on residential care continued despite its high cost and the demographic trends and studies (from as early as the Phillips Report, 1954) that warned of the escalating financial and resource consequences of an ageing population.

Case study

Jonathan, a man in his early 60s, introduced earlier in this chapter, has moved from a large institution of over 300 people with 'mental handicaps', located on the outskirts of the town, to a small supported living flat in the centre of a major city, where he lives with a degree of independence managing his money and able to hold a small job in a local café. One of the issues for Jonathan is that he often feels alone and isolated.

Long-term care summarizes both care in institutions (nursing and residential) and at home and is mainly concerned with personal care, such as bathing, dressing, shopping, preparing meals, nursing and rehabilitation. The scope of such services, eligibility criteria and the emphasis on each of these components however have altered over time, with a greater emphasis now on people needing multiples of these rather than single components such as domestic services. The shifts have proved to be controversial. Eligibility, access and assessment are three areas where the boundaries have shifted. Access to residential and nursing care depends on an assessment by the local authority plus a financial assessment and it is this latter component which has become increasingly the focus of tension.

Eligibility for services at home has also proved a source of tension as preventative services such as cleaning or shopping are only provided to people with complex and multiple personal care needs. For example, targeting through multi-professional assessment has left many older people without services. There has been more home care since the NHS and Community Care Act (1990) but it has been targeted at the most dependent. Prevention has been squeezed out. For Jonathan extra low-level support would not only be helpful to keep his flat clean, but it could have prevented admission to hospital following several falls that happened when he tried to clean his windows.

The 1990s was characterized by increasing targeting of services to those people in greatest need. In response to the multiplicity of assessments under health and social care a single (Wales) or unified (England) assessment to determine needs was established. However, a lack of consistency between local councils in their provision of services to older people with similar needs has led to the government introducing national eligibility criteria, Fair Access to Care (DoH, 2002), in England. Four bands describing differing levels of risk have been constructed: critical, substantial, moderate and low. The Department of Health guidance on setting eligibility criteria within *Fair Access to Care* states that 'councils should prioritise needs that have immediate and longer-term critical consequences for independence ahead of needs with substantial consequences. Similarly, needs that have substantial consequences should be placed before needs with moderate consequences; and so on' (DoH, 2002, p. 5). This is increasingly an area of tension and debate. The withdrawal of domestic help is an issue which many people and professional bodies (such as the Association of Directors of Social Services) are opposed to, feeling that the boundaries have shifted too far to be helpful in preventing 'care' and dependency. Two of the key issues are the inadequacy of provision and variable quality of domiciliary care. A number of studies show that people feel they are not getting enough services or that there are gaps in the services they receive (for a comprehensive review see Social Care Institute of Excellence (SCIE), 2005).

A more holistic approach is needed which considers all the social needs of older people including transport, housing, leisure and recreation. A 'Third Way' was heralded by the 1997 Labour Government with an emphasis on independence and user voice heralded through the 1998 White Paper *Modernising Social Services* and through an emphasis on integration, joined-up government, partnership, and whole-system approaches, exemplified through the Better Government for Older People 1997 initiative working across policy areas.

The mixed economy of care

One area however that has had far reaching consequences but where there was little public debate has been the shift from public to private sector services.

Care within a 'welfare paradigm' (Jones, 1998) was universal, collective and comprehensive, centralized and characterized by all the elements of institutionalism – dependency, compliance and the constraint of professional freedom by institutional regulation. Care under this notion meant 'being cared for' in an objective way. Ideological and philosophical debates about the shift from a welfare paradigm to a market paradigm in the 1980s and 1990s have dominated the arena of care.

Over the last twenty years national governments (both Labour and Conservative) have followed a market approach. In policy the state has withdrawn from direct provision, to rely on the market and private and voluntary organizations to provide (and private finance to pay for) welfare services. There has been pressure on local councils to use privately run services rather than develop their own. Markets and competition were at the forefront of Best Value with an emphasis on targets and performance (for example, the National Service Frameworks for Mental Health (DoH,

1999b) and Older People (DoH, 2001) have continued with this approach). This has been more apparent in adult services than child care. The independent sector, under contract by the local authority, has provided an increasing volume of homecare services; contact hours rose from 5 per cent in 1993 to 64 per cent in 2001 with the consequent fall from 95 to 36 per cent of public sector provision (Forder et al., 2004).

The main changes were initially spearheaded through the NHS and Community Care Act 1990. Successive Conservative governments' dislike and suspicion of local authorities came from a number of perceptions, for example that local authorities were expensive, inefficient and unresponsive to the needs of the consumer. Welfare pluralism was seen as a solution. The rise in the private sector and diminution of the state sector in provision of care was the major outcome of this approach.

Consequently the private (for profit) sector has grown considerably. There was a revolution in care in the 1980s with massive expansion of residential and nursing homes fuelled by a change in social security payments. This proved alluring to local authorities as it meant that highly dependent older people could be paid for from the social security budget rather than from social services departments. This was much more attractive than spending money on refurbishing their own care homes to meet new regulatory standards or to close homes, which would be politically unacceptable. Small providers in this sector provided most residential places for older people and about a third of residential places for young people. Increasingly, however, in relation to older people multinational corporations are entering the scene. In child care services the trend is for private companies to train foster carers.

In health care compulsory competitive tendering, clinical audit and managerial control were hallmarks of the change to a market paradigm of care. Rationing came to the forefront, based on age and waiting lists. The purchaser–provider split became evident through the roles of NHS trusts and general practitioners as health providers, and other large general practices and health authorities became fund holders. Patients became consumers, with notions of choice. Care in the community became de-professionalized with an emphasis on self-care. Contracting determined the definition of 'care'.

Long-term care shifted therefore from a public to a private responsibility with little debate (Player and Pollock, 2001) about such commodification of care. The concept of care was reframed by commercialization, targets and contracts and pushed to the margins of state provision.

A barrage of legislation on social care was introduced following the Labour victory in 1997. A greater emphasis has now been placed on partnership and devolving social care down to a local level. This is seen through a number of initiatives such as Better Government for Older People. This also formed part of their 'Third Way for social care' as an alternative to a return to the ideology of the public or the private sectors. The emphasis was placed on quality rather than who provided.

The roles of the family and the state

One of the central debates over the last forty years has been the respective roles of the family and the state in the provision of care. The bedrock of care has predominantly rested within the family, with the state playing a subsidiary, rather than complementary role (see chapter 4).

Different countries and cultures have different norms and values in care. The Scandinavian countries, traditionally seen as providers of universalistic services, have been limited in recent years through the lack of public funds to support such provision, yet there is still a notion of collectivized care. For example, in Denmark parental rights in relation to day care provision for children mean that women are able to juggle work and family life. In Norway, family care is provided alongside state care with the notion of independence as primary. The Scandinavian example illustrates that a straight substitution effect cannot be assumed between public and private provision of care and both may coexist side by side supporting each other.

The middle and southern European countries range from those Mediterranean countries where care is still 'privatized' among the family, to the Bismarckian state such as Germany where care is 'privatized' through voluntary provision and Beveridgean countries such as England with a mixture of public and private provision in care.

In the UK the policy approach is to preserve people's independence (although in later chapters this will be debated as a contradiction of policy and practice). More preventative care services will be needed (intermediate care) to enable people to 'live at home for as long as possible', which has been a mantra of successive governments since the 1970s. Other policies in the UK such as direct payments influence care and give users the option of choice in the market. In relation to community care the state viewed care as a private concern and only intervened when the family was not able to provide it. Increasingly the state's role is being replaced by that of the market, with the state now intervening when the market fails in its standard of care and through regulation. The concept of care is increasingly being privatized through a shift back to the family on the one hand and the market on the other.

In relation to child care the responsibility was that of the mother and a private matter until the Children Act 1989 cast child care as 'children in need' into the welfare arena. Working mothers on the other hand were engaged in childcare and were framing childcare in a consumerist model rather than as a welfare issue. Consequently those children in the 'looked after' system under the Act were stigmatized. Under New Labour's approach to poverty care has been reframed in terms of social pedagogy through the Sure Start initiatives that put care back into community and family arenas.

Informal versus formal: paid versus unpaid

The term 'mixed economy of care' is misleading as the bulk of care comes from the informal sector, from friends, family and neighbours. During the 1970s, the idea of care being undertaken *by* the community, instead of just *in* the community (Bayley, 1973) came to underlie much of the thinking about community care. This paved the way for a detailed exploration of what informal care was about, and who undertook this care. From the 1980s onwards there was a vast amount of research undertaken. There were also notable policy developments in the UK, beginning with the NHS and Community Care Act 1990, the Carers (Recognition and Services) Act 1995 and the Government's National Strategy for Carers 1999, followed by the 2000 Carers and Disabled Children Act and the Carers Assessment and Carers (Equal Opportunities) Act 2004.

Informal and formal care are also not perfect substitutes (Pickard et al., 2000; Motel-Klingebiel, Tesch-Roemer and von Kondratowitz, 2005). The relationship between them is finely balanced as any diminution in care in one sector has implications for the other. Any changes in financial benefits to carers or direct intervention or rationing of formal care as well as general social and economic policies will have consequences for the informal sector (Walker, 1993). With the plethora of providers in the independent, private and voluntary sectors it is not simply the relationship between family and state that has to be considered.

Research shows that state intervention doesn't undermine family care. In Scotland for example the introduction of free personal care has not reduced the level of informal caring (Bell and Bowes, 2006). Informal care is often taken to its extreme before formal care is asked for. Yet those living within family situations have in the past been deprived of services.

Twigg and Atkin (1994) describe four models which looked at the relationship between formal and informal care through the relationship of social care agencies with carers, seeing carers as:

- resources
- co-workers
- co-clients
- superseded (the aim here being to replace current informal care relationships either in the interests of the person being cared for, or in some cases to enable a person to give up caring).

Twigg and Atkin argue that as resources, carers are 'taken for granted' and social care agencies are present to fill the gaps. To encourage support from carers and keep them on board incentives such as support groups and information for carers are provided as part of the 'package of care'. As co-workers carers are seen as semi-professionals, yet the power imbalance between carer, care recipient (who is absent in the relationship with the social care worker) and the worker is not one of equals. The third model of co-client creates an additional category in need of care. Much of the literature on carers has framed carers in this light with the emphasis being on the stresses and burdens they face in the caregiving duties (Schneider et al., 1999; Bauld et al., 2000). A significant influence on legislation on care has been the burden and stress that carers face.

In a critique of this emphasis on the negatives in the caring relationship Nolan, Grant and Keady (1996) suggest that what is needed is a working model that more adequately reflects the goals of partnership and empowerment inherent in policy and practice guidelines and recognizes the power differentials of formal service provision and family care. In this they advocate the carer as 'expert' in their caring relationship, knowledge of the person cared for and in their coping skills. The focus here is on the rewards of caring. Yet carers may feel caught between their status as 'experts' and the need for support.

Paying for care

Financing of care is complex and such complexity has led to a number of contentious issues around the notion of care. One debate has been around the 'funnel of doubt' of the ability to pay for increasing numbers requiring care.

Funding continuing care: the long-term care debate

The current system of pensions, disability benefits and care services involves a mixture of money benefits (cash) and benefits in kind (care). Eligibility rests on assessment of need, which in many cases requires professional judgement. It is however a confusing system. Such a complex funding system (from the NHS, local authorities and from the social security system) has grown up piecemeal and haphazardly. It contains a number of funders and providers each with different management or financial interests which can work against the user. It has shunted the costs of care from services which were free at the point of delivery to more means-tested provision (from health to social care). The National Health Service, being funded from general taxation, is free at the point of delivery, whereas local authority services are means tested. The different funding schemes operated by the two have led to a lack of coordination and integration. The difficulties also stem from the complexity of provision through the mixed economy, with the split between purchaser/provider, public/private, and which services come under health and which under social care responsibilities.

The difficulty surrounding this issue has been one of shifting boundaries between health and social care while there has been a lack of movement in funding. More recently the introduction of intermediate care and care trusts in England has attempted to bridge this divide. Hospital discharge is a key illustration of this point (see chapter 8). Waiting times and throughput in the acute hospital sector have been subject to targets set by the Labour Government. Local authority social services were seen to be responsible for delaying discharge from hospital thus cascading failure in meeting targets throughout the system. As a consequence intermediate care services were introduced to prevent admission as well as provide rehabilitation. In addition, from 2004 local authorities were charged if older people were not discharged after their acute treatment had ended. This narrow focus on integration has not however led to a more inclusive and broader vision of the care that is wanted or needed by older people themselves and risks the 'revolving door' syndrome if there are no corresponding investments in long-term support (Glendinning and Means, 2004).

The issue of the costs of care and who pays has tended to focus around the debate on long-term care for older people. People resent having to pay for care by releasing their assets and support for state funding is strong, yet this is far from the picture of long-term care, particularly in England and Wales.

In 1999 the Royal Commission on Long Term Care proposed that all of the costs of nursing and personal care in care homes and personal home care should be met by the state out of general taxation. Only 'hotel' costs were to be subject to a means test. However this was rejected in England and payment for personal care operates in care homes and domiciliary settings. The Welsh Assembly Government, the Northern Ireland Assembly, along with the Department of Health for England, unlike Scotland, have not introduced free personal care. Charging for home care is still set locally. Since 2002 nursing care is provided free across the UK.

Many people expected social care, like health care, to be provided free and now have a sense of a 'broken' contract with the state. Charging for services has a long history, dating back to the 1948 National Assistance Act. Yet this has become a contentious issue, the focus of much debate. There is a widespread sense of injustice and unfairness about the way long-term care is arranged and funded. A small number of people face 'catastrophic' risk – all their assets are at risk from means testing. Most people accept that they should make some contribution toward care costs, but do not think it is right that they can end up with virtually nothing to show for years of work and saving. The issue is a political one of what it is reasonable to ask individuals to pay toward their own care.

Evidence so far from Scotland (Bell and Bowes, 2006) indicates that eliminating charging can support personal care sensitive to individual needs and has improved equity particularly for those of modest means and people with conditions such as dementia.

The funding crisis has had severe consequences for the private sector. Caught between punitive local authority charging limits and care home standards, many home owners feel pressurized (Netten, Williams and Darton, 2005). In Lincolnshire the gap between what is considered an economic fee and what the council is prepared to pay was in 2002 running at £2,000–£5,000 per month depending on the level of care necessary. Many homes in the private sector are facing bankruptcy. Consequently few private owners are investing in good quality stock and there is under-capacity in many areas (Netten, Darton and Williams, 2002). There are severe consequences for older people who have to move; particularly if they are suffering dementia they will be moving from familiar surroundings without choice and in a potential state of vulnerability. Although the government has no stated policy about moving people into the private sector, this is being driven by other measures, including the Treasury's refusal to fund improvement to local authority homes. However a change in perception by people as to whether they need care services will alter the equation. The next generation of older people may have a totally different disability profile, with disability compressed into the few years before death. Programmes to prevent disability could significantly affect costs. Similarly the balance of care shifting to more home care will reduce long-term care costs. Successive generations of older people may also have larger occupational pensions and more over the age of 85 will own their own homes. These trends may result in individuals making greater personal contributions to long-term care costs, thereby limiting the cost to the public sector. However not everyone has a private pension and it is increasingly likely that this will be a minority of the population. For others who can afford to, efforts may be made to leave as much as possible to the next generation rather than save for long-term care.

Hancock (1998) sounds a cautionary note in that 'it would be wrong to think that home ownership alone can solve the problems of income poverty in old age either now or in the near future' (p. 29).

The long-term care debate is still ongoing following the 1999 Royal Commission on Long Term Care yet the government has brought in a number of initiatives to divert attention and to broaden the nature of the debate. There is an emphasis on intermediate care (DoH, 2000) rather than long-term care with the objectives of reducing avoidable admissions to acute beds, facilitating timely discharge from acute beds, promoting effective rehabilitation and minimizing premature or avoidable dependence on long-term care in institutional settings. The emphasis is on prevention, which is not necessarily a cheaper option and not necessarily in the form of the early intervention services that people require.

Direct payments

A paradigm shift to new models of care however is taking place, giving people more choice about their care arrangements through direct payments. This can be viewed as part of an improved culture to allow choice over the nature of support, when it is provided, by whom and at what level. The increasing focus on independence and empowerment, promoted through policy, has meant an emphasis on users as care consumers in the last decade. One of the main ways of empowering users has been through direct payments.

Ungerson argues that the dichotomy between paid and unpaid work (informal and formal care) is breaking down through such 'marketisation of intimacy and commodification of care' (Ungerson, 2000, p. 69; 1987; 2004). Ungerson proposes a typology of payments, examples of which can be seen in a number of European countries and the US:

- caregiver allowances paid through social security and tax systems
- proper wages paid by state or state agencies
- symbolic payments paid by care users to kin, neighbours and friends
- payment of volunteers by voluntary organizations and local authorities
- routed wages paid via direct payments to care users (2000, p. 71).

The impact on the care relationship, Ungerson argues, will be different in each category. Care allowances, although based on the principle of citizenship, lock carers into the relationship, preventing them from 'paid' employment. Examples of 'proper wages' in Scandinavia for example suggest that carers in an employer–employee relationship may be locked into an isolated dependency relationship (Lingsom, 1994). Baldock and Ungerson (1994) in reviewing the third type suggest that payments made by users out of their benefits lack the rules of reciprocity and have no established boundaries, for example in relation to time, and therefore workers risk exploitation. For both remaining types the relationship will lack the personal exchange and intimacy between carer and user, based on a long history or biography, as workers are locked into a contractual situation to guarantee reliability and control. In terms of routed wages,

> These developments constitute the sharp end of commodified care and marketized intimacy. The underwriting, by the state, of employer/employee relationships within the care relationship dyad is, at least for European welfare states, a radical innovation in care delivery, apparently reversing the professional and bureaucratic hegemonies in health and social care developed since World War II. (Ungerson, 2000, p. 79)

In her 2004 article Ungerson looks at further types, for example additional flows into the household, common in Austria and Italy, where money can be spent on anything within the household and goes unregulated. Additionally the 'grey' market is made up of foreign migrants, undocumented, with low wages and no employment rights. The complexity of care arrangements, payment and the impact on relationships can be far reaching and can lead to exploitation and blackmail. Yet her evidence suggests that in some instances informal carers behaved in exactly the same way pre- and post-payment, leading her to conclude that 'routed wages' are not necessarily well suited to the management of social care. Direct payments may also be yet another example of shifting responsibility away from the professional to the individual for their care, thus de-professionalizing social work and social care. Additionally such payments, whether to the carer or to the person requiring care, are substitutes for formal care; for example in Norway where the public sector is declining, payments move responsibility for provision to the 'private' arena of care.

On a positive note, Daly and Lewis (2000) argue that through direct payments to people receiving care a new type of welfare citizenship may emerge based on citizenship-based entitlements. Land (2002) argues that the use of cash payments in the informal sector is not detrimental to the willingness and ability of carers to care and through such policy both love and money can coexist in the care equation.

The aforementioned tends to assume that domiciliary services are available to choose from, yet there are still significant costs to carers themselves.

Costs for carers

The burden/stress literature dominated many of the earlier debates on care. Part of this burden included financial costs to carers (Rimmer, 1983; Ginn and Arber, 1994). Increasingly the debates have focused on the employment costs of caring (Phillips et al., 2002; Evandrou and Glaser, 2004). Growing numbers of women and men are working longer hours alongside their caring responsibilities. The impact of care on employment can take a variety of forms – lost career opportunities, missed hours and meetings, stress and a lack of confidence in returning to work (Phillips et al., 2002). For carers the pension penalty of caring is also significant. The impact of caring responsibilities upon financial well-being can last well beyond the period of caring itself. Employment across the lifecourse is crucial in building up pension rights. Carers whose work arrangements are affected by caring responsibilities can suffer both a 'wage penalty' and a 'pension penalty' in later life (Evandrou and Glaser, 2004). In an earlier article by Evandrou and Glaser one in five midlife women who had ever cared reported stopping work on starting care responsibilities, another one in five reported restricted hours or fewer hours and earned less money (Evandrou and Glaser, 2003). The costs for carers go far beyond economic costs, impinging on their social, psychological and physical well-being (Keeley and Clarke, 2002).

In conclusion there are a number of issues around the provision and funding of care that lead to new debates within policy. The provision of care is now distanced from the state in both child care and, in particular, care for older adults (Cameron, 2003). The key question is how far the emphasis on welfare pluralism will go and what role local authorities will play in this, given that services in England are shifting, particularly for older people, to the control of the National Health Service and for children's services to education and new combined agencies like Connexions. The shift toward privatization is irreversible and current debates are about how far this can go. To what extent the public sector should shoulder the costs of care is a continuing question.

New partnerships however are evolving in relation to care and new players are appearing. Local employers and communities are entering the field with a different concern around the notion of 'care' – that care for employees and their dependents equals productivity. We have in the last five years seen the return of philanthropic attitudes of employers toward day care provision on site for children and even older adults, together with a government emphasis on encouraging this development through parental leave, 'granny leave' and benefits to carers.

In relation to funding, conceptually we need to reframe our welfare system, acknowledging that the shift to individual responsibility charted in the Thatcher era is likely to continue. This is despite opposition to the assessment of assets in the access to long-term care. The system is riddled with inequalities not only in terms of who gets assessed under the NHS or for local authority help and hence how each is funded and whether people have to pay; there are also geographical inequalities, not only between Scotland and England but between local authorities that use different criteria for assessments (SCIE, 2005).

Alternatives to funding can include insurance-based schemes which are not effective immediately. In effect the present generation would be required to fund the care costs of several generations and this could polarize society, yet the long-term care insurance industry has not taken off.

There are outstanding questions that need debating, one of which is how much emphasis we should place on quality and how much on cost. It was assumed that targeting would lead to an improvement in the quality of care yet this is still to be evidenced. The debates on long-term care primarily centre on a concern for 'cash limited public expenditure' (Means, Richards and Smith, 2000, p. 167) rather than the quality of the experience for residents.

Choice has been a mantra used to justify a number of the shifts in 'care' policy. This however may be a myth as people with few resources can only choose between services which the local authority has contracted in the private and independent sector. Only very few people receive direct payments. There is also an issue of supply with the independent sector residential and nursing home market restructuring to stay in business, thus changing the nature of provision from a small family-run enterprise (Phillips, 1989) to one of a multinational corporation, with a medical model emphasis (Holden, 2002).

In reviewing social policy Henderson and Forbat (2002) argue that social policy has missed out the relational component of informal care, and in so doing has dichotomized the 'carer' and 'cared for' in policy. This has been reflected in terminology used, again highlighting the lack of agency in the care relationship, the narrow focus on the carer and the continual strategy of focusing on one part of the care relationship in policy and research, making the 'cared for' invisible. They also argue that policy 'circumvents people's own meanings of informal care' (p. 677) and ignores the interpersonal dynamics of a relationship which is often the most valued component of the interaction rather than the provision of care itself; 'the meaning of care provision is thus subsumed by the interpersonal' (p. 678). This interpersonal component also allows for emotions to be expressed in contrast to a professional care relationship, yet policy ignores emotional support in the relationship and consequently devalues the informal side of caring. Interpersonal relationships require time for listening, without which entire areas of need may be neglected. In response they call for a relationship-based social policy. Care in such a policy context also needs to be holistic. A set of tasks or policies can be introduced but leave a person 'malnourished'; for care to be 'good enough' all needs have to be addressed.

Connections between the macro policy world and the individual at the micro level also need to be considered by practitioners working in the social care field. Despite the pursuit of independence as a policy goal, as Jonathan illustrated earlier, isolation and loneliness can be major factors. Similarly on an individual level the policy move toward direct payments may result in lack of choice if resources are not available to choose between.

The changes highlighted above and the issues of quality and cost all lead to a lowering of expectations in care provision and financing from the state. It is timely therefore to re-evaluate the concept of care and consider how we revive it in the public arena. That debate is yet to be conducted. It is important however that new models of care are created rather than relying on existing models which have led to serious provision and cost problems.

4

The Care Relationship: Do Families Care?

Chapter 3 looked at the development of policy around care in the community, yet the definition of community is just as complex as that of care and has a number of different meanings. Community care has been associated with care *in* the community, predominantly stressing the location of care, until Bayley (1973) highlighted that care was *by* the community, with most caring activity being undertaken by families and other 'informal carers' in the community. 'In practice care by the community equals care by the family and in practice care by the family equals care by women' (Finch and Groves, 1980, p. 494).

Chapters 4 and 5 expand on these statements and ask whether families still do provide care to their members – raising debates over obligation, duty, love and solidarity – and who within families provides care. Chapter 5 questions whether we can still hang on to a gendered notion of care.

The concept of care has been synonymous with 'the family' in its broadest sense and a hierarchy of norms and obligations regarding who should care has operated. As Twigg (1998) comments, 'families have always been the main source of help to older people' (p. 128).

It is on the basis of the centrality of the family in caregiving that policy is focused. In many European countries the principle of 'subsidiarity' forms the bedrock of all policy responses to care with the family seen as the natural carers and the first port of call for assistance. The welfare state has a residual role as a safety net.

In the UK the Griffiths Report (1988) and subsequent legislation (NHS and Community Care Act 1990) highlighted the primary role of families and the need to support them. This has also formed the basis of legislation relating to parenting in the Children Act (1989), Child Support Act (1991) and Family Law Act (1996) and is embodied in the Sure Start programmes supporting parents in deprived areas and Every Child Matters (DfES, 2003); all reinforce the notion of parents working in partnership with the state, voluntary and commercial organizations to ensure opportunities for care and protection of children. The 'best interests of the child' has also held centre stage in family policy, not only in the Children Act 1989 but also through the UN Convention on the Rights of the Child. Right-wing thinkers and others in the 1980s and 1990s also reinforced this through a number of publications in relation to the need for mothers to stay at home to provide proper socialization of their children, the importance of a father figure and a male wage, and reinforcing the duty to care for older relatives (Green, 1994; Cockett and Tripp, 1994). Embracing the family as the primary caregivers also stemmed from the notion that this policy would be a cheaper option than institutional care. The family has therefore been central to community care and child care debates.

Whether families still care is a question that has been asked through the centuries. Since biblical times the question has been asked 'Am I my brother's keeper?' (Genesis 4, verse 9) and through the commandments we are required to 'Honour [our] father and [our] mother' (Deuteronomy 5, verse 16). However in more recent times the debate has been generated through policy concerns such as the availability of the supply of care and the debate about individualism in late modernity, rather than a concern for carers per se.

In the 1950s and 1960s despite the policy steer to 'keeping older people at home for as long as possible' and the belief that people were best placed within their families (Vaughan-Morgan, Maude and Thompson, 1952) there was also a groundswell of opinion that the willingness of families to take on such obligations was diminishing. This was reinforced by studies looking at hospital admission and discharge (McEwan and Laverty, 1949; Thompson, 1949) and by professional bodies such as the Geriatric Almoners Group (Means and Smith, 2000) and was considered by the Phillips Committee of 1954. The old question of whether the family cared raised its head again in sociological debate in the 1950s.

This was the backdrop for studies such as Sheldon's *The Social Medicine of Old Age* in 1948; Townsend's *The Family Life of Old People* in 1957; Young and Willmott's 1957 work *Family and Kinship in East London* and Shanas et al.'s *Old People in Three Industrial Societies* in 1968. These studies all found that the family was strong in its provision of care and support for older people. The argument then developed to look at how the state could support the family without taking over its functions (Moroney, 1976).

Qureshi and Walker in their classic study *The Caring Relationship: elderly people and their families*, published in 1989, highlighted the situation from both sides of the care relationship. They found that families were 'thriving' and 'operating very effectively to deliver tending and support when it is needed' (p. 244).

In more recent times, one of the reasons for such a frequently asked question is based on the changing structure of the family and its consequences. What or who is in the family and how are definitions of family changing? Chapter 3 outlined the main drivers of change that have fuelled policy responses. In relation to the family there have been specific changes:

1. The growth in divorce, reconstituted and step families, and new forms of family life (gay and lesbian households) all have implications for intergenerational relationships and care exchanges. Traditional notions of obligations and duty are changing as a consequence. In the last thirty years divorce rates have doubled and there has been a similar increase in the proportion of children living with a lone parent or with cohabiting parents.
2. Traditional notions of the nuclear family with 2.5 children and the male breadwinner are no longer sustainable. Average family size in the last thirty years has decreased from 2.9 children to 1.6 children. The decline

in fertility rates is accompanied by the postponement of childbearing and an increase in childlessness.

3. Feminization of the workplace: women's wages are increasingly important for household resources.
4. Geographic separation: families are more dispersed, having to move with their jobs. Husband and wife may both commute long distances on a daily basis, entailing substitute care for children for long hours during which they are separated from their parents.
5. Postmodern emphasis on individualism and selfishness of modern families has led some commentators to conclude that there is a decline in moral values and commitment to care.
6. There is increasing concern over issues such as individual rights, citizenship and quality of life and consequently the acceptability of current levels of family responsibility and the quality of life of family carers (Salvage, 1995).

Older people themselves have been found to support the thesis that family care is declining (Walker, 1993). But does this mean the family as a unit of care provision is under threat? Can we – and should we – rely on families? What role do families play in providing care?

Williams (2004) suggests caution in claiming that the family is disintegrating or that 'close relationships are being democratised. The old exists in the new and the new in the old' (p. 24). It is the variability of how people experience family life that is captured in empirical studies.

The family in the social network

Research into care of adults has traditionally looked at the role of families by asking who provides support to whom; research methods often assume that families care and ask who in families provides what care. More recently social networks have been drawn on to measure the nature of care and who provides it. Locating families within networks is a fruitful way of looking at their contribution to care vis-à-vis other actors. It is often these other actors or supporters of the primary caregiver that get ignored in the care literature.

Exploring social networks is a useful tool in investigating the dynamics of family care. Social networks are defined as

> a set of linkages among an identified group of people, the characteristics of which have some explanatory power over the social behaviour of the people involved. It is the set of people with whom one maintains contact and has some form of social bond. Social support is defined as the interactive process in which emotional, instrumental or financial aid is obtained from one's social network. (Bowling et al., 1991, p. 549)

Case study

Consider the following family tree of relationships.

Edgar and Maria (who is now deceased) have four children, John, Julia, Susan and Jasper. John and his first wife, Connie, have a son Sebastian; subsequently John and Connie have remarried and each has additional children. Julia is in a long-standing lesbian relationship with her partner, Pat. This caused several disagreements in the family and Pat and Edgar do not speak to each other. Pat and Julia have an adopted daughter Suzanna. Edgar's other daughter Susan is single and rarely visits as she lives in the USA. Jasper is married to Betty and they have four children (Terence, Nigel, Chris and Pamela).

Edgar has severe arthritis and suffers from bipolar disease which he has controlled for most of his life. Connie, John's first wife, still lives locally and continues to care for Edgar having developed a close 'father–daughter-in-law' relationship with him when Maria was alive. Her role as a carer has evolved and she feels committed to continue caregiving despite being divorced from Edgar's son. Jasper and Betty also live locally and regularly engage their children in running errands and visiting Edgar as well as providing day-to-day meals and transportation. Julia has a history of ambivalent relationships within the family and although she was the last to leave home she rarely provides any support to Edgar. John is very disabled and his son Sebastian provides care for him when he can. Recently he has not been doing well at school and has become withdrawn creating disharmony in the family. Connie is annoyed that Sebastian is missing school because of his care duties. She is also finding it difficult to juggle her work and care for Edgar and resentment is building towards other family members who 'could be doing more'.

For practitioners working in this situation and reflecting on the concepts introduced in this chapter, there are a number of issues: Who will provide care in the future for Edgar, Julia and Susan? Can a large diverse family network contribute to care in a coordinated and planned way? Will care fall to one member, with little support from others? What role does gender, proximity, family history and marital status play in assessing the situation? Are there sexist and ageist assumptions among family members about who should provide care, and how do social care workers tackle this?

Studying social networks has a long history stemming from the work of Elizabeth Bott in 1950. Social networks extend beyond the family yet families are important within them. Network analysis however does not make any prior assumptions about the relationship types within them and who does what for whom.

A social network technique is used by Kahn and Antonucci (1980) to establish the closeness of individuals to the person. Their network diagram of three concentric circles allowed them to ask people to place in the inner circle people who are 'so close and important that they cannot imagine life without them'. Those less close but still important are listed in the middle, and so on. Respondents are subsequently asked about the support functions of the people listed as well as other socio-demographic data. In using this technique numerous studies have shown that a family is central in providing care to its members.

In a study by Phillipson and colleagues (2001) looking at the family and community life of older people in urban areas the mean size of networks was 9.3, with women having larger networks than men. Few older people were isolated and the majority had close relationships. Within these networks it was clear that close relatives dominated (forming nearly three-quarters of the total). Children were particularly important in both giving and receiving support. Within the immediate family daughters were most significant. Nearly 70 per cent of respondents reported confiding in daughters about issues of concern. Daughters also appear to be of importance particularly to mothers, as they were in the studies in the 1950s and other more recent studies (Jani-Le Bris, 1993). Willmott and Young in the East End in 1957 noted that 'mothers and daughters are each other's constant companions and helpmates' (p. 75).

In the late 1990s, with the changes to family life and particularly the increasing working routines of women, one mother recognized the changing demands on the family: 'My daughter comes in and phones me, we communicate with each other every morning at 9.30am . . . My daughter is very good to me but she leads her own life' (Phillipson et al., 2001, p. 164).

In providing instrumental support there were fewer children available, reflecting geographic distance; for almost half of the respondents who had children who would give help, most was left to one child. It is the immediate family rather than the extended family that play a significant role in providing support.

However, recently questions about the caring capacity of these networks to initiate and sustain high levels of care are being debated. What is known about the characteristics of social networks that might enhance their transition from social and support networks to care networks? Can networks of people who provide general support develop into networks that provide personal care?

Recent work on care in Wales (Wenger and Keating, forthcoming), the Netherlands (van Tilburg, 1998) and Canada (Keating et al., 2003) highlights certain features of support and care networks. Size is not a good predictor of whether care is provided or who provides it (van Tilburg, 1998); composition; density, including strength and continuity of ties, for example as spouses or children (Antonucci and Akiyama, 1987); normative expectations to provide support (family are more likely); and reciprocal relationships (important for the maintenance of friends in the network) are however important. Characteristics of the care recipient also are likely to influence membership of the support network: those who are older, unmarried, childless and in poor health are least likely to have robust support networks (Keating et al., 2003).

Care networks are consequently smaller and more family-focused than support networks. Generally only a few members of the network provide care and different members provide different types of care depending on their relationship to others in the network, for example spouses first provide personal care. Proximate support network members are more likely to provide direct care than those at a distance. Empirical evidence from the studies above shows that over time the network becomes smaller with more narrowly defined functions. This has led to the conclusion that it is the care dyad that is crucial in caregiving relationships (Boaz and Hu, 1997). If friends are present in the care network they are likely to be on the margins or are old friends (Keating et al., 2003). Yet it is increasingly important to study care networks in their own right (Wasserman and Galaskiewicz, 1994) rather than focus on a particular dyadic relationship, as care is often not a simple one-to-one relationship. Drawing on our case study, if Edgar were to be asked who he would place as 'most important' in his social network circle then Connie may be the person he chooses; similarly it may be Connie who is the only person providing intense hands-on care to Edgar with support from Betty and Jasper being marginal.

Why do families care?

We often say 'blood is thicker than water' because of marital, biological and emotional ties but this doesn't explain all the dimensions and reasons for caring, for example why women do most of it.

How people in families become carers and the hierarchy of care has been explored by numerous early writers in this area. Finch and Mason (1993), Ungerson (1987) and Lewis and Meredith (1988) all explore the process by which one member of the family takes on caregiving. Such studies found that the hierarchy depends on gender, perceived priority role of certain members, proximity, marital status, other caring responsibilities and mutual affection. Often it is left to a main carer with little external support (Rodriguez, 1993; Green, 1988; Wright, 1986). Lewis and Meredith (1988) in their influential study of mothers and daughters found that few carers actually make the decision consciously but drift into caring because they are already living with their mother or they thought it was a 'natural' stage in their lifecourse and 'obvious'. The definition of 'care' for these respondents was not a conscious one but intuitive, moving through stages which they termed as semi-care to full care. Shared histories, ongoing relationships, reciprocity, knowledge of preferences and values of the family members were important in the care relationship.

There had been a long-held assumption that family care was provided out of duty, love or obligation. The literature on carers was primarily dominated (particularly in the US) by a number of studies emphasizing the lack of individual choice and agency as well as the stresses and burdens on carers without unravelling any positives in the caring experience.

However further studies have demonstrated that networks of affection are negotiated and moulded by individuals rather than through fixed obligations and rules or by blood and marriage. Finch (1995) argues that families do not operate under the concept of 'fixed obligations' through marriage or birth. She argues that the responsibilities which people feel and acknowledge toward their relatives are more complex and individualistic; they are more akin to 'commitments' which are developed over time on the basis of reciprocity, individually negotiated rather than conforming to a particular role or genealogical line.

Love, duty, power, guilt, reciprocity (Ungerson, 1987; Qureshi and Walker, 1989) and altruism (Grant and Nolan, 1993) can characterize the care relationship within families, as well as a lack of alternatives. Many carers may feel they have no choice or that it is part of their identity to care. Many women may be pleased to be in a nurturing and supportive role and find many positive rewards from caring (Grant and Nolan, 1993). Carers can see their responsibilities as 'payback' for the care they received as children or as a 'bank' of reciprocity for their own future care needs.

In the case study, Betty is employed on a part-time basis as a care worker in a residential establishment. She sees herself as Edgar's carer and has tried to resist pressure to take on more of his care from other family members who see her as the one 'experienced' in providing care and as 'someone who would know what to do in an emergency'.

So far this chapter has concentrated on community care in relation to adults and has related to extended family members. Caring for children is firmly located in the policy framework of the nuclear family. Kinship networks are central to good outcomes for children, even when children are unable to live within these networks. Maintaining contact with family is crucial to psychological and emotional well-being. The Children Act 1989 embodies the principle that 'where possible children are best brought up within their families'. Because of this social workers are instructed to work in 'partnership' with families (Saleeby, 1997). The family remains the key holder of information regarding attachments, identity and heritage. It is also a basis for children's self-esteem and competence (Ward and Rose, 2002). A 'family strengths approach' is now a common feature of current mainstream developments within child care services. These factors are influential in policy, for example Sure Start (Home Office, 1999), in which one of the desired outcomes is to strengthen families. Kinship care, involving grandparents as carers, has also increased as grandparents live longer healthier lives and have fewer grandchildren to care for. In general grandparents are acting as carers when parents work, get divorced or when a parent is unable to care through illness or drug abuse (Bornat et al., 1999).

Structures and forms of family life for children have become more complex. 'Different families, family relationships and consequently different forms' (Allan and Crow, 2000) have grown yet children appear to have an accepting, inclusive view of what counts as family and their definition does not centre on biological relatedness or 'nuclear' norms (Morrow, 1998). For children the family is increasingly both the nuclear and extended family with relatives remaining the primary source of support to children.

Williams's Care, Values and Future of Welfare (CAVA) study (2004) found that in relation to the well-being of their children, parents negotiated 'the proper thing to do' in and through their commitments with others, whether these commitments were in relation to dissolved marriages, non-resident partners or transnational kin. 'The picture of self-actualising pioneers or selfish individuals fails to capture the moral texture of family lives and personal relationships in Britain today' (Williams, 2004, p. 41). The choices that women make in relation to work–life balance are not free 'preferences' but are embedded in moral considerations about what is right for their children. The choices that mothers make to return to or enter the workforce are not simply preferences but negotiated on the basis of what they see as being a 'good mother'. Such commitments are influenced by identity, sense of belonging, social networks and local circumstances.

> In working through their dilemmas, certain practical ethics emerge . . . which enable resilience, facilitate commitment and lie at the heart of people's interdependency. They constitute the compassionate realism of 'good enough' care. They include: fairness, attentiveness to the needs of others, mutual respect, trust, reparation, being non-judgemental, adaptability to new identities, being prepared to be accommodating and being open to communication. (Williams, 2004, p. 74)

Williams (2004) advocates a political ethic of care (see chapter 5). Whereas citizenship is based on the ethic of work she argues that the ethic of care must be central to any concept of citizenship. The heart of the argument centres on interdependence, viewing care as a meaningful activity in its own right and being attentive to others (p. 76). This not only applies to adults but to children, as respect for children as citizens is part of this ethic, providing them with opportunities for involvement in their local communities and giving them a voice. Policy makers, she claims, have ignored the importance people have attached to care and commitment: people have not lost their moral values nor are they totally motivated by money, but care is invisible and not valued.

Disaggregating care in the family

In the 1990s the debates around caring began to 'disaggregate' the notion of carer and care, breaking it down into different types of carers and the varied nature of the caring task. Certain groups and individuals within families were identified with specific care issues. On the policy scene the difficulties of young carers were highlighted (Becker, Aldridge and Dearden, 1998) along with the problems surrounding working carers, juggling paid work and care for older people (Phillips, 1995). The longevity of families has also raised issues around care for people with a learning disability (Grant, 2001) and, with reconstituted families increasing, care in gay and lesbian families (Manthorpe, 2003). The concept of care has been reframed in relation to each group.

Young carers

Prior to the 1990s a population of carers under the age of 18, looking after a sick or disabled relative, remained hidden in policy and academic debate (Heal, 1994). Much of the discovery of this group of carers has focused on their prevalence and the restrictions in their lives imposed by caring responsibilities. Policy responses are embodied in the Children Act 1989 and the Carers and Disabled Children Act 2000. Issues raised by young carers in relation to their experiences of caring can be similar to those of carers of any age, such as dependency, lack of training, disrupted or nonexistent social life and gendered expectations. However role reversal can come early for young carers as they take on parental tasks and different roles in relation to their siblings, as in the case study in relation to Sebastian. How caring might affect future life chances is a particularly important issue for this group compared with older carers. The concept of care is here related to education and transition to independence.

Working carers

Here the concept of care has been reframed as a concern of employers in relation to productivity, recruitment and retention of employees. Demographic change has altered family structures resulting in a 'sandwich generation' of middle-aged women caring for both children and older parents. Such women are also likely to be in the workforce. Policy across Europe has recognized this change, and the reconciliation between family and working life and the responsibilities for family care within this balance have been considerations for many European countries. Support for families has included paying carers to stay at home, state-funded childcare provision, policies at the workplace, and provisions for mothers and fathers to share care and work through generously paid parental leave arrangements, as in Sweden. Employers are found to be much less sympathetic when care of older people is part of the equation (Phillips et al., 2002), but there are a number of initiatives such as the UK government's work–life campaign and various employer policies and practices that are useful to carers. Take-up of arrangements is low and often depends on how good relationships are between the worker and their manager.

Caring for someone with learning disabilities

Medical and technological advances have meant that people with learning disabilities are living longer than in previous generations. Increasingly we are seeing older parents care for adults who may have challenging behaviour. In one study family caregivers aged 60 and over were responsible for looking after 44 per cent of all adults with a learning disability who were living in a family home (McGrother et al., 1996). The ability to continue caring, concerns about the future of their son or daughter and about being 'perpetual parents' (Tobin, 1996) are key issues.

The debates in this area have centred on rights and choices and the independence of people with intellectual disabilities as well as the appropriate role of the state in supporting both parties. One of the continuing difficulties has been social exclusion. The principle of 'normalization' (Wolfensberger, 1980) was first developed in relation to this field; social systems theory has also been applied (Bogdan and Taylor, 1989), stressing the importance of the relationships that people with learning disabilities have with others. Grant (2001) discusses the approaches that have been adopted in relation to older people with learning disabilities, which include a social well-being approach (Bach and Rioux, 1996) 'seen as conditioned by self-determination, equality and democratization' and Renwick and Brown's (1996) opportunity-constraint model, where quality of life is viewed in terms of 'being, belonging and becoming' (p. 158).

Developing theoretical approaches

If we are to understand the complex and diverse intimate family relationships in societies undergoing rapid social changes, we require conceptual and theoretical lenses. Throughout the years there have been a number of theories used in practice around the family in relation to care of children (for example, attachment theory) and adults (for example, role stress theory).

A development in relation to intergenerational family care has centred on the 'solidarity' and 'conflict' debate. In the US Bengtson and Roberts (1991) proposed the solidarity model, an intergenerational model with six dimensions: structural (opportunities and barriers), associational (integration and isolation), consensual (agreement and dissent), affectional (intimacy and distance), functional (dependency and autonomy) and normative (familism and individualism), collectively termed as 'solidarity' (Bengtson et al., 2002, p. 571). The model has two dimensions:

- structural–behavioural (associational, functional and structural)
- cognitive–affective (affectual, consensual and normative) (Bengtson and Roberts, 1991).

It serves 'to characterize the behavioural and emotional dimensions of interaction, cohesion, sentiment and support between parents and children, grandparents and grandchildren, over the course of long-term relationships' (Bengtson, 2001, p. 8). The paradigm has been widely used by family researchers to study parent–child relations in various ethnic groups (Markides and Krause, 1985; Kauh, 1997) and cross-national contexts (Katz et al., 2003b; Knipscheer, 1988; Lowenstein et al., 2003; Marshall, Rosenthal and Daciuk, 1987; Morioka et al., 1985; Phillips, Ogg and Ray, 2003).

The theoretical framework of family solidarity was criticized during the 1990s on the grounds that the term 'solidarity' indicates an emphasis on consensus and idealization (Marshall, Matthews and Rosenthal, 1993; Lüscher, 1999). The conflict model has been introduced alongside, yet it is recognized that family relations can contain elements of both solidarity and conflict. The theoretical framework of family solidarity and conflict was challenged again in the late 1990s when a new concept, 'family ambivalence', was introduced for studying parent–child relations in later life (Lüscher and Pillemer, 1998; Connidis and McMullin, 2002; Lettke and Klein, 2003).

The empirical relevance of the concept is confirmed in a number of studies, for example in relation to divorced and gay and lesbian relationships (Lüscher, 2003; Connidis and McMullin, 2001) and in relation to parental care by young German adults (Lorenz-Meyer, 2003).

Ambivalence in caring relationships is not new. It has long been highlighted. Evers in 1985 observed that the mother–daughter relationships she studied were 'fraught with ambivalence'. The nature of care can also influence the dynamics of family care and create ambivalence. There are often assumptions that the care recipient is grateful for care provision from families, yet people with certain mental health problems may see their problems as stemming from within the 'supportive nest' of the family. People with learning disabilities may not be able to achieve autonomy and may face conflict relationships with their parents (Walmsley, 1996). There may be ambivalence when there is a desire to care alongside increased female autonomy and expectations of equal opportunities (Brody et al., 1983). The voices of carers juggling work and care can reflect such ambivalence.

Changing relationships: care outside families

Changing family forms and the embracing of diversity within families have not only broadened the definition of the family but have also opened up the way for the study and discussion of the role of non-kin in the care relationship. Friends can be an important source of care. Dorothy Jerrome (1981) points to the crucial links women have with friends. In the study of urban areas Phillipson et al. (2001) found that particularly for those without children friends provided the greater part of support. Even if children were present friends and neighbours played significant roles, yet did not stray into areas involving intimate and personal care. It was only in the absence of available family members that friends took on these tasks. Pahl (2000) argues that there is considerable blurring between family and friends in people's lives, particularly in relation to commitment. In the case study Pat and Julia have a number of friends who are committed to sharing their care if and when the need arises.

Across Europe families still play an important role in care for their members, even in states such as Denmark where the state assumes an important role.

Family interdependence is still a major factor in societies undergoing change. Other forms of 'family' are emerging and friends are increasingly taking on importance in care tasks. The typical 'caring' family no longer predominates – there are many families with many configurations of care. The complexity of relationships within families makes it impossible to be categorical about who depends on whom.

A continuing debate first raised by Finch and Mason in 1990 concerns the personal preferences for care – between the family's contribution and that of 'formal' providers. In Qureshi and Walker's study (1989) most people preferred existing family help even if a home help was available. Arber and Ginn in 1991 devised a hierarchy of care preferences where spouse care was first, care by peers second and children third. In a five-country study Daatland and Herlofson (2003) highlight the north–south dimension in the support for filial norms with the highest in Spain and Israel and the lowest support in Norway, England and Germany. However 'filial solidarity is not incompatible with generous welfare state arrangements, nor do filial obligations necessarily imply that the family is seen as the "natural care provider"' (p. 537). Additionally in all countries there was a call for more state responsibility. The family therefore appears to be alive and well but demands on the family through modernization and globalization continue to raise the debate about the sustainability of its role in the care relationship.

The Future of Family Care was the title of a book edited by Allen and Perkins in 1995; in it several authors explored the demographic trends that might predict the future. Most of the debates on the future of care centre on the availability of supply and the demand for care. These are influenced by changes in the form and function of families and relations within them, which will continue to change.

The projections suggest that up to 2031 or so the numbers of dependent elderly people receiving informal help with domestic tasks will increase faster than those not receiving it. The proportion of dependent elderly living alone may also fall slightly as cohabiting (older people living together outside a traditional marital relationship) becomes acceptable. As children become dependent for longer on their parents through high costs of housing and education and families have children later in life there will be considerable implications for reciprocity across generations. The implications will be widespread – socially, economically and politically. Families are now global and the repercussions of family care in one country can have an impact on another. Care is therefore a global concern and has to take prominence in debates across the policy arena. If equality is a realistic plank of policy then giving equal weight to an 'ethic of care' and an 'ethic of work', as advocated by Williams (2004), shows a way forward. In relation to Edgar's situation everyone should have the opportunity and choice to care. This is again taken up in chapter 5.

5
Changing Gendered Notions of Care: Is Caring Still a Feminist Issue?

Numerous studies and books highlight the gendered nature of care. From popular fiction (for example, Margaret Forster's *Have the Men Had Enough?* (1989)) to social care practice and policy (for example, past criteria for Invalid Care Allowance payments) the assumption is that women primarily provide the bulk of caring for children, disabled adults and older people.

Yet questions raised by the early feminists such as Graham, in answer to Ungerson's question 'Why do women care?', exposed the gender inequality in care.

> Caring defines both the identity and the activity of women in Western society. It defines what it feels like to be a woman in a male-dominated and capitalist social order. Men negotiate their social position through something recognized as 'doing', based on 'knowledge' which enables them to 'think' and engage in 'skilled work'. Women's social position is negotiated through a different kind of activity called 'caring', a caring informed not by knowledge but by 'intuition' through which women find their way into 'unskilled jobs'. (Graham, 1983, p. 30)

Ironically it also reinforced the notion of a gendered view of care and shaped the way in which policy has developed. Policy has hinged on notions of dependency, of 'us' and 'them', the carer and care recipient, viewing women in private domestic roles with men as the main breadwinners in the public arena of work.

Although this may be an outdated model for the twenty-first century, in practice such stereotypes still persist. A more recent view has emerged that calls for the repackaging of the concept of care based on a 'feminist ethic of care' which places it in a democratic citizenship mould, pervading all aspects of human life and the lifecourse.

This chapter seeks to outline the historical development of the feminist debates on care, primarily as they relate to care of adults. In addition it will look at the evidence we have of men's contribution to caring. Pervading the debates are the notions of citizenship, obligation, rights and responsibilities which have revolved around the concept of an 'ethic of care'. This liberating concept is seen as inclusive, embracing gender integration rather than exclusion and segregation and can be developed as a guide for policy and practice. The chapter concludes by assessing whether care is still a feminist issue.

The development of care as a feminist issue

Feminist theorizing is still one of the most significant areas of development in critical approaches to care and caregiving. As a number of authors (Calasanti, 1993; McMullin, 1995; Estes, Biggs and Phillipson, 2003) stress, 'gender itself is a crucial organising principle in the economic and power relations of societal institutions as well as of the social life throughout the lifecourse' (Estes et al., 2003, p. 44). No one feminist perspective encompasses the diversity of women's experiences and consequently, although the gender lens is still of relevance, it is important to broaden the debates to incorporate race, age and class. Such diversity, however, was not recognized by the early feminists.

Gender became a political issue in relation to the concept of 'community care' in the UK in the 1980s. Carers were positioned centre stage in the promotion of 'informal care' in the 'mixed economy of welfare'. Policy makers presented community care as a step to independence but for feminists it reinforced the dependence of women. Policy of the time was premised on the notion that women were the natural carers in the family, locked into domesticity, while men supported them through the labour market. The needs of the labour market governed much of the thinking behind policy in relation to the family. The introduction of the Invalid Care Allowance (ICA) reinforced this, paying carers (apart from married or cohabiting women who were assumed to be caring anyway) of older people if they were unable to be in the labour market. The campaign to extend the ICA to married women, together with a number of small studies (Lewis and Meredith, 1988; Nissel and Bonnerjea, 1982) that showed the predominance of women in the caring role, led to the interest of feminists in the issue of caring. Finch and Groves in 1983 looked at how community care policies were built upon the assumption that women were both available and willing to care for frail older people and kin. They extended Bayley's (1973) statement 'Care in the Community equals care by the family' to 'equals care by women'. Other studies highlighted the burden and stress that carers faced (Nissel and Bonnerjea, 1982; Parker, 1985; Levin, Sinclair and Gorbach, 1989; Braithwaite, 1990).

Although many of the feminist studies looked at small samples their findings were politically potent. Most carers and recipients in their studies were older people and there was recognition that the older person's vote was important and growing. Such pressure led to the inclusion of a question on caring in the General Household Survey (see Green, 1988). Additionally many feminists were themselves experiencing caring responsibilities.

Underlying a policy perspective there were a number of assumptions: that women were the key to stability in family life; that they were natural carers; and because caring was a domestic task it followed that it was women's responsibility. Commentators such as Fisher (1994) concluded that this perspective underestimates the stressful experiences of carers and reinforces gender stereotypes in caring. It also views men who act as carers as something unnatural, a 'Mr Wonderful', whereas women are simply expected to cope. 'Normal gender roles' stigmatized, romanticized and conveyed sainthood on men. A number of studies provided evidence of this. Wright

(1986) in her study of single carers found that frail older women would struggle to maintain their role as housekeepers when living with their unmarried sons, but this was not the case when they were living with unmarried daughters.

Mansfield and Collard (1988) show how easy it was for women to slip into traditional roles once married. Some research (Blaxter, 1976) has shown that when men leave hospital they expect their wives to care for them and professionals collude with this view. Consequently service provision to this group has been poor. Finch and Mason (1997) also detailed how this role may even continue after divorce or separation.

The arguments at the time revolved around the labour market and the work ethic. Women's caring roles restricted them in the labour market and the low pay that women received, especially where they were in part-time work, didn't allow them to pay for good quality alternative care. The feminist goal was to liberate women from this so that they could become self-sufficient and independent in the labour market. This work ethic has continued to dominate the concept of care and resulted in gender division.

The analysis of gender, employment and informal care suggests that personal relations, marital relations and class relations are gendered processes through which involvement in caring takes place.

Case study

Sabrina has three children and looks after her sister with cystic fibrosis. She relinquished work when her first child was born and has not considered or had the opportunity to return to work. In the 1960s and 1970s this would not have been an unusual scenario, yet it was not until then she realized how stressful she had found balancing the needs of her children with those of her sister and how much her work had meant to her. To Sabrina caring was 'something she had to do', providing meals and personal care for her sister that had to fit within school hours. Her husband sorted out the finances for the household and although he had parents who were very frail he found himself in a very different position, with social services supporting them through day care and meals on wheels to enable him to remain in employment.

Second wave feminism

The second wave feminists of the 1980s also questioned the conceptual underpinnings of gendered care. They argued this from a different perspective to the first generation of feminists, taking the view that men and women's caring experience was different and their motivation and ability to care differed. On this premise they celebrated women's difference.

Ungerson (1987) made the distinction between *caring about* and *caring for*, with men emphasizing the former and women the latter. It was argued that caring involved not only physical tasks but also emotional responses and these elements were gender-specific. Men and women identified different definitions and meanings of care based on their experience (women = practical and emotional; men = financial and managerial). This is aptly summed up in Forster's book *Have the Men Had Enough?*

> I would say dad and Stuart and Adrian seem to enjoy peace of mind where Grandma is concerned. Dad hasn't got peace of mind about the money he's forking out but that's different. He doesn't worry about Grandma. Mum lies awake at night, fretting. Bridget is screwed up all the time with anxiety and pain. The pain is because she truly loves Grandma. (Forster, 1989, p. 19)

Chodorow (1978), Gilligan (1982) and Graham (1983) all identify basic differences between men and women, locating the technical and emotional capacity to care in the experience of mothering, and suggest that women are more morally adept at recognizing need. Gilligan (1982) suggested gender differences in the moral framework in which men and women operate, with 'men's moral frameworks underpinned by a notion of rights that are subject to public and rational assessment, women's being underpinned by a notion of responsibility, which are assessed in relation to individual circumstances' (Williams, 2001, p. 476). The argument around 'emotional labour' (Hochschild, 1983) and Graham's 'labour of love' (1983) captured the unique mixture of love, affection, duty and hard work that characterizes women's caring. Women's identities were shaped by their caring roles. Caring shifted from a focus on labour to women's identity and how they saw the world.

The concept of 'difference' was promoted by the work of Wærness (1992) who coined the phrase 'rationality of care' as a way of expressing the content and qualities of caring. In carework she claims it is rational to look after other people's needs and this demands 'head, heart, hand coordination'. This is a rationality which according to Wærness is carried out by women in their everyday lives. She argues that female and male versions of rationality are different. Men see it as being autonomous and independent of others with the masculine world bounded by individualism, sense of self, a wish for power, action and agency. Intimacy and emotion are not part of the male established organization; formality and distance are seen as the way to rational decisions. Impersonality comes in the form of professional detachment, for example the bedside manner of the male doctor. Calasanti (2003) argues that such conceptions of masculinity enable men to separate out 'caring for' and 'caring about' and to detach emotion from instrumental tasks as a buffer to stress.

By contrast, for women there is a continuing experience of connection with others, a focus on interdependence and a sense of self in reference to others. Gilligan (1982) argued that a woman's identity is entwined with that of others and gains from the private world of relationships. She described this as the female ethic of care as opposed to the male ethic of justice, which promotes rights and individualism. Men's perspectives are characterized by 'doing' (although this is restricted to tasks other than personal care) whereas women's are by 'being', men's lives being less involved with emotion.

Critique of the early feminist writers on care

There have been a number of criticisms about feminist perceptions in both waves of feminism. Unpaid carers were invisible to feminists in the 1960s and 1970s and consequently there is an absence of first wave feminist analysis in the care of older dependent adults (due to structural rather than individual causes) (Hooyman and Gonyea, 1995). The feminists' early focus was on issues related to younger women (childbearing, freedom and self-expression) and little attention was paid to the caring functions of the family (Dalley, 1988). Debates around care focused on mothering originally. Some debates conflated mothering with caring and treated them together (for example, both are locked into low pay) but there are differences between mothering and caring, for example around education, age, the labour market and differences in caring for children and adults.

Care issues were seen as gender-neutral or just a women's issue, acceptable and 'natural'. There was little recognition of sequential or consecutive periods of care for children or older relatives and the impact this had on all other aspects of work and family life. Lives of older carers were ignored, particularly at the end of their economic life in paid work. Age was ignored in the debate; older people were seen primarily as care recipients, dependent and powerless (Finch and Groves, 1980). Disabled people were cast in the same mould.

Secondly, an overemphasis on gender (generally within marriage and nuclear families) to the exclusion of other factors, such as age, sexual orientation, race, class and ethnicity, led to a criticism of the feminist paradigm. Feminists also did not look at how these interacted across the life-course. Even in terms of gender there are many different kinds of women in different care situations that went unrecognized. Women also have multiple identities, other than that of caregiving, but initial analysis was confined to the domestic sphere of their lives. Women from ethnic minorities provide such an example. Different age profiles for example in ethnic minority families and different social construction of family responsibilities combined with black people's experiences of racism lead to specific and unique experiences of caring.

The feminist analysis of caring and definitions of women's care tended to highlight the subjective stress and burden faced by caregivers and focus on the individual rather than the needs of women as a group. Such theorizing led to interventions which were addressed toward women themselves, such as counselling, and this may have inadvertently blamed women for the burden they faced rather than seeing it as a structural or systematic failure.

Seeing care as a burden also pathologized older people and led to ageist attitudes that all older people required care and were burdens on society. This has been challenged by numerous critical gerontologists (Walker and Phillipson, 1986; Phillips, 2000).

A further critique of early feminist writing focused on the argument that carers faced double jeopardy because in the main they were women and secondly they were older (considerable care being provided by older people). This supported the argument that you can't look at carers without looking at those being cared for. Disabled people also give as well as receive care and the early feminist view can place people being cared for in a dependency relationship. There was a view which reinforced the belief that disabled people were passive recipients of care and a burden requiring protection. The 1990s therefore saw the disability movement (consisting of activists as well as academics) challenging the concept of care and taking account of the differences in power relations between cared for and carers (see chapter 2). The conflict between users and carers in this sense dominated community care debates.

Increasingly there has been diversity rather than convergence in feminist writing since the early work in the 1980s. This has resulted from the emergence of challenges to the white ethnocentrism and ageism of much of the feminist writing and the backlash against feminism from opponents such as those from the New Right, for example Green (1994) and Morgan (1994). The New Right argued that women should be the main carers within the family and not the breadwinners. It promoted the traditional nuclear family (Green, 1994; Morgan, 1994) and argued that feminization of the workforce had adverse effects on the ability of couples to found and maintain families. This became implicit in social policy, particularly community care legislation, at the time.

More recent feminists seek a deconstruction of the concept of care and a deconstruction of the public masculine world that gives it shape. Tronto (1993) cautions about such distinctions on the grounds that caring includes both emotion and practice; emphasizing emotion sentimentalizes and privatizes care (people do not share their emotions as readily and women undertake this side of caring); and limiting men's caring to the rational aspects of care reinforces gender stereotypes.

Responses to the gendered nature of care

Dalley in *Ideologies of Caring* stressed collective solutions to the problem. Bringing to bear a feminist perspective defines caregiving as a societal, not an individual responsibility. Dalley (1988) argues that 'A feminist vision of the society assumes collective responsibility for all its members, values the activity of caring and recognizes the worth of those cared for and those performing the caring' (p. 67).

Dalley argues that the principles of collective care are validated by the notion that dependence and interdependence are facets of all human relationships. Individuals are not forced into care, dictated by their biological connectedness, but can make and be responsible for their own decisions about caring and their life choices. Consequently the individual can organize a network of care and relationships based on free choice, recognizing the strengths that all individuals bring to these relationships. In an ideal collectivist arrangement the system of care should be responsive to the needs of individuals receiving care and dependent people should be economically secure.

While feminist commentators calling for collectivist care initially subscribed to institutional care, those from disability groups found the argument hard to accept. Similarly a rejection of the homogenization of collectivism followed, stating that we need to recognize the heterogeneity of care, acknowledging that the care needs of a young disabled person will be different from those of an older person with dementia, where dependency may be the only accessible form of care.

The disability critique focused on the *rights* of carers (carers' assessments; carers' special grant; right to number of days off work for caring; protected pension rights). This perspective has led to a debate which can be described as the third wave of feminism.

Third wave feminism

Estes and co-authors (2003) suggest that we are in stage three of Matthaei's (2001) conception of feminist economic transformation, distinguished by gender integration. This would involve 'valuing the feminine' and the integration of 'caring into the economy (stripped of their negative, subordinated qualities)' (p. 465). Such feminism is based on a rights perspective which Stone (2000b) describes as the right of families to care for and be helped to care for their members; the right of paid caregivers to give humane, high quality care without compromising their own well-being and the right of people who need care to get it (Matthaei, 2001). It can be argued that these rights should be not only recognized but legitimized in policy. Such snapshots of care have led to what has been termed third stage feminism embracing gender integration.

The ethic of care

Another response to the gender debates has come from philosophers and political scientists (Tronto, 1993; Sevenhuijsen, 2000). The earlier gender binary argument that women are characterized by the ethic of care and men by the ethic of justice (Gilligan, 1982) has been replaced by more complex understandings that go beyond biological determinism. The concepts of inclusion, citizenship and interdependence have provided a different perspective on the concept of care, one which is not locked into the earlier dichotomies between public and private, male and female notions of care. The key features of such a position are that:

- care is central to all human life; it is a social process and a daily human activity
- caring is seen as a moral orientation, as an ethic that guides human agency in a number of fields

- individuals exist in a complex arrangement of social and care networks and relationships, where 'the self can only exist through and with others, and vice versa' (Sevenhuijsen, 2000, p. 9); care is an integral part of these networks
- different perspectives of care receivers, caregivers and policy makers are taken into account; difference and diversity are embraced
- notions of collective activity and citizenship should be an integral part of the concept of care (Sevenhuijsen, 2000)
- care should be seen as an activity and a disposition (Tronto, 1993)
- caring should be a valued human practice
- interdependence is part of citizenship
- it challenges the false dichotomy between carer and cared for
- it recognizes choice
- it is a political concept (Williams, 2001).

Fisher and Tronto (1990) propose four dimensions of care, each corresponding to a value and forming the basis of an 'ethic of care': caring about – noticing the needs of others and being *attentive*; caring for – taking *responsibility*; the activity of caring ('maintaining and repairing the world' and 'carrying out the daily activities of care') requiring *competence*; and, fourthly, care receiving, involving an awareness of one's vulnerabilities and interaction of *responsiveness*. Based on this they argue that care is central to all our lives and is something we all experience (Tronto, 1993).

In this way care is seen in a more positive light, not focused on stress and burden for carers or seen as a barrier to self-fulfilment and an autonomous life. An obligation to care enshrined in legislation, such as that in Germany in relation to long-term care or in Malaysia around filial care, would not be necessary.

Similarly it is a debate which attempts to break the link between those who work and those who are not in paid employment. An ethic of care extends the boundaries beyond the labour market. This paradigm of care values all those involved in care. Lloyd (2004) illustrates the importance of the ethic of care to the discussion of dependency and care at the end of life, recasting older vulnerable and dependent people at the end of life as citizens with rights. Rights in this context are conceptualized differently from care and should not be based on work.

She questions the notion that older people at the end of life are able to assert their rights in relation to death when their rights in old age have already been diminished. In embracing a feminist ethic of care Lloyd argues that a new conceptualization of equity, justice and autonomy can be advanced, differing from the perspective of those who emphasize the individualist approach. The feminist ethic of care stresses the collectivist approach and social context linking those who care to those cared for. The needs of those at the end of their life should be considered in relation to their connectedness to others as well as their rights as individuals.

The main critique of the ethic of care has come from disability studies. Silvers (1995, 1997) argues that disabled people are cast into a need and dependency role and a position of incompetence. The ethic of care also does not take into account the power inherent in care relationships. The caregiver's morality derives from the incompetence of the care receiver. One of the ways to counteract this is to take a relational perspective, one argued for by Wendell (1996), where both carer and care recipient would be engaged in the moral basis of care. Interdependence and reciprocity are more helpful ways in describing this relationship and can act as a 'discourse bridge' that will mediate between the disability studies and feminist perspectives on care (Watson et al., 2004, p. 331). Drawing on the work of Fraser (1989) and his conceptualization of interdependence based on needs that are ongoing, anticipatory and immediate, Watson et al. (2004) argue for an emancipatory approach that they term 'caringscapes' (McKie, Gregory and Bowlby, 2002). Thus caringscapes would involve many, if not all, of the following activities or experiences (Watson et al., 2004):

> planning, worrying, speculating, prioritizing, ensuring quality of care, accessing care, controlling, paying for care, shifting patterns of work, job (in)security, the potential for promotion, moving home, managing family resources,

supporting school work, being involved in the school or care group, and so on. (p. 341)

Conceptualizing care in this way brings together needs and interdependence and can link both feminist and disability groups together. A reconstruction of interdependence is a theme which Williams picks up in her discussion of a political ethic of care. As Williams (2000) argues, the 'work ethic' has pervaded our analysis of care. This is evident in the ways care has been conceptualized: from the early feminists who conceptualized unpaid work as labour that could be tied in with the formal economy (care preventing women from entering the labour market) to the later analysis of women balancing paid work and family life and thirdly the gendered discussion of the paid care workforce. The arguments have extended not only to the nature of unpaid care but also to the paid arena of care provision. Paid and unpaid care is intertwined (Oakley, 1974). For many women their care role extends across paid and unpaid, private and public roles through formal and informal care.

The concept of care in the workplace and work–life balance or juggling (Bernard and Phillips, 2007) provides an important space which Williams claims for arguing a political ethics of care (Williams, 2001). Within this debate there has been a premium placed on time rather than money as women juggle different and overlapping spheres of their lives. Although policies have been introduced to support this, for example the National Carers Strategy 1999, Williams argues that political values that support such policies have to be explicit; in terms of childcare the emphasis has been on the work ethic and productivity, enabling mothers to return to work for example. As she argues, no political principle about care equivalent to that of paid work exists.

Gender and work are also intertwined with the paid care workforce; domestic skills have long been associated with work in the formal care sector. Women often occupy roles in the paid workforce which require emotional labour (Hochschild, 1983). Gattuso and Bevan (2000) argue that the dynamics of mother–daughter relationships dominate caring practices in care for the aged.

There has been a growing recognition of the economic exploitation of women as paid carers in nursing and in home care. Low pay and poor career progression have historically characterized women's carework. Men who were in the care workforce functioned at organizational and managerial level rather than in direct service provision, reinforcing the concept of the 'rational' man fulfilling a technical role rather than using the interpersonal skills required at the level of the individual. Similarly the involvement of men in child care framed as protection cast them in a legitimate protective role, the equivalent of which did not exist in relation to older people.

Williams (2001) advocates a new political ethics of care, one which would balance the ethic of paid work, enshrined in much social policy around community care and work–life balance issues. She proposes three strategies for achieving this – reframing around personal time and space, care time and space, and work time and space. Prioritizing people's lives around these three concepts can be liberating and 'allows us to prioritise the opportunities to give and receive care and to normalise responsibilities for giving care and support and needs for receiving care and support' (Williams, 2001, p. 489).

The arguments about the deconstruction of gender and the blurring of public and private spheres of life can be highlighted in practice by two areas: the greater visibility of women in the labour market and the increasing role of men as 'informal' carers.

Reviewing our case study from an ethic of care perspective we find that Sabrina and her husband John would face a different situation. Good quality social care provided by the state would enable Sabrina to return to work should she wish; John would also have the option to reduce his hours and be more flexible to provide care for his parents, children and sister-in-law should he wish to do so. Their lives would be organized around care time, personal space and work time. Under Williams' reconceptualization they would be able to prioritize their time around care as a main function. Social services would play a role in supporting both partners in providing care interchangeably with care provision being seen as a major right and responsibility.

Increasing role of men in caring activity

Male caring is often seen as an anomaly (Orme, 2001) yet evidence is accumulating to demonstrate that it is far more widespread than assumed. The 1985 General Household Survey (GHS) and its analysis by Green in 1988 showed that although caring was gendered it was not in such a global way as feminists had made out. Of 6 million carers, 40 per cent were men, tending to be spouse carers. Bytheway's 1987 study of steelworkers in South Wales showed they took on exactly the same roles as women, suggesting that we need to re-examine our theoretical framework, and study care within particular cultural contexts.

Male caregiving was largely hidden in the initial debates because it is generally apparent at older ages with spousal care predominating. The older the couple the more likely the man is to be undertaking care. The large proportion of men caring for spouses in older age was illustrated by the 1992 GHS, showing that overall 10 per cent of women and 6 per cent of men were carers; however, over the age of sixty-five the figures were 13 and 14 per cent respectively. Some would argue that such caring is done out of duty to the marital relationship (Orme, 2001).

Family structure and class also influence whether men care. Canadian data (Campbell and Martin-Matthews, 2003) show that men providing personal care are more likely than other men to have no siblings. Education, income and occupational status also play a part; working-class men who have never left home may be in a powerless position with fewer resources to 'resist' the caring role. Middle-class men have more resources and for men it may be power over resources which determines whether they take on the caring role. Fewer gender differences are found on the basis of class once caring begins. In terms of employment, both middle- and working-class men are likely to find that care responsibilities affect their jobs and career prospects.

However, even with men's increasing involvement in care, gender stereotypes still persist. In childcare, for example, the presence of men in the nursery was no guarantee of a less gendered nature of care (Cameron, 2003). What is necessary according to Lister (1997) is a shifting in the sexual division of labour. One way of changing 'men's behaviour and their relationship with the public and private spheres is to enforce caring work as a public citizenship obligation just as paid work is' (p. 179). An alternative is to articulate citizenship in terms of 'right to time to care' with measures to back this up particularly for men, for example by regulating hours. Such policies exist in Sweden in relation to both parental care and care for older parents, but for wider application, changes in the workplace and in employment cultures are necessary.

Blurring the boundaries between public and private is crucial in any conceptualization of care and citizenship (Ungerson, 1995). Women as mothers and carers operating in the private sphere and spaces of home and community have to be enabled to participate on equal terms with men in the public sphere of the labour market. Lister (1997) argues that policies to shift the balance for men and for women are central and 'until women become centre stage in policy debates their citizenship is likely to remain marginalised' (p. 194).

Sharing care between men and women can lead to more equity in community care. As policy makers recognize the erosion of the male breadwinner model and the emergence of the dual earner model, policies must be developed that allow both men and women to choose and engage in shared care. However, integrating an inclusive perspective across policy areas poses several challenges. One challenge is to move away from the focus on individualism to a collectivist approach, where care is valued. Such concepts will be picked up in chapter 8 in professional debates in care; they will, however, need to be challenged if an ethic of care is to take centre stage in our thinking.

Is care a feminist issue? Some conclusions

This chapter argues that we cannot either be gender-neutral in our analysis of care or use a gendered lens to see the concept as a 'women's issue' but should advocate gender integration as described by Williams' (2000) political ethic of care.

In part Williams' ethic of care was inspired by the Scandinavian conception of care, which between 1960 and 1975 focused on the aspects of relationship and promoted a solidaristic, interdependent and rights-based equality notion of care (Rose and Bruce, 1995; Hirdman, 1998). Care was not kept on the periphery of public life. Yet economic crises have seen a loss of jobs for women and greater inequality in Sweden. Moving the concept of care to Williams' notion of a political ethic of care would begin to insure against such a reversion.

In reviewing the history of feminism and care in this chapter we highlight some of the issues for social care professionals today. The historical debate has had great influence on the carers' movements and the way the debate has been translated into practice, for example the early feminist view that care was a burden stigmatized older and disabled people and led to assessments based on ageist and sexist assumptions. The challenge for practitioners in health and social care today is to embrace a new conceptualization of care based on the ethic of care and to develop assessments based on these principles. The difficulty is balancing this with the needs of the agency and bureaucratic demands to form fill and manage limited resources.

There is a crucial need to move these debates from the theoretical to the practical. In practice and policy terms society is a long way from recognizing the values of such an ethic as practices continue to differentiate and reinforce stereotypes in who does what for whom and to reward individualism and independence. The importance of interdependence and shared vulnerability is crucial to the progression of the debate. Care is a feminist issue but needs to be broadened to incorporate and engage all members of society.

6
Culture and Ethnicity: Is Care Culturally and Ethnically Sensitive?

'Care' has been scripted from a Western perspective with the predominant literature focused on an ethnocentric view of care. The literature in the UK in relation to ethnic minority care has taken on three distinct but linked areas: the patterns of care within ethnic minority groups in the UK, which draws on descriptive, small-scale, mainly local qualitative studies; the relationship between ethnic minority groups and the state through the provision of services and professional practices; and thirdly and more recently, critiques of the approach to the concept of race, ethnicity and care, advocating a multicultural perspective. Consequently the corresponding debates have centred on particular myths highlighting issues of whether minority ethnic groups 'care for their own' and whether services are appropriate and sensitive to the needs of ethnic minority carers. A third area of debate has centred on what approaches professionals and others should be utilizing in delivering care. Issues around asylum seekers, travellers and illegal immigrants will increasingly challenge our views on these issues. The shifting cultures and identities of these groups challenge our predominantly ethnocentric notion of care.

This chapter traces the arguments and ideas in relation to these three areas of interest. It does not attempt to be exhaustive in its coverage but draws on a range of research to illustrate the main debates and issues.

In relation to children there has been considerable debate around issues such as mixed race adoption (Thoburn, 2000) and the number of children from ethnic minorities in the care system (Barn, 2006). Studies with children from black and minority families illustrate diversity across ethnic groups as a common theme. Children from Indian and Pakistani groups and those from mixed race backgrounds tend to come to the attention of social services younger than white children. Black children are disproportionately represented among children 16 years or older. The Children in Need (CIN) data (2001) also show that compared to other ethnic groups there is a high proportion of disabled children from Asian backgrounds. Children of mixed race and black backgrounds are more likely than others to become known to social services because of abuse and neglect. Children of Indian, Pakistani and Bangladeshi origin are more likely to come into care through disability (SCIE, 2005). Thoburn and colleagues (2004) in a major study found that it was 'how' not 'what' services were provided that was crucial. Different approaches to information about parenting styles and aspects of social work that are associated with successful placements were needed for different groups. This was overlaid by the complexity and centrality of interpersonal relationships in children's social care services.

This area of study has been brought to the forefront by concern about the number of children from ethnic minorities in the 'looked after' system (Lees, 2002) and breakdowns in the community care system in relation to psychiatric patients from minority groups, brought to public attention by incidents such as the stabbing of Jonathan Zito by Christopher Clunis (see chapter 9). The main thrust of this chapter however concentrates on social care for older adults.

The acknowledgement of culture, race and ethnicity in the arena of 'care' has been relatively recent and mainly followed from the development of community care. Care literature before the 1980s makes very little reference to ethnic minority care in the UK.

Although debates about the needs of ethnic minority groups and appropriate provision of services have grown, there has been relatively little theorizing of care. Where this has occurred it has tended to follow mainstream theorizing along gender or feminist lines. Yet there has been a growing number of descriptive studies and texts on ethnic minority groups and community care (Blakemore and Boneham, 1994; Ahmad, 1996; Phillipson et al., 2000; Gunaratnam, 1997b, 2004). Some of this has been a by-product of interests in other areas such as migration, settlement and race relations (Ahmad, 1996), which have been 'radicalized' topics of debate, ignoring ethnicity and culture (Blakemore, 1997). Similarly, only recently there has been theorizing based on comparison of perspectives from country of origin (Burholt and Wenger, 2003).

Before settling into this chapter it is imperative to define terms which are often misused and confused in studies. Culture 'can be taken to embrace all things that distinguish a way of life. Ethnicity can incorporate culture but also implies a political identity' (Blakemore, 1997, p. 30). This may be through language, religion, belief or claims on land. 'Race' is often used interchangeably with ethnicity but it is more problematic as 'it entails the idea that the human population is made up of biologically different groups' (Pilcher and Whelan, 2004, p. 132).

Debates focusing on 'myths': ethnic minority care in the UK

The invisibility of the needs of ethnic groups is reflected in the paucity of research and writing about this area of work compared to other discourses of care (see the amount on burden and stress for example, or care for dementia sufferers in white families). Some would argue that there has been a total neglect of cross-cultural and comparative perspectives (Blakemore, 1997), particularly when compared to the number of studies in the USA.[1]

Looking at the demographics of care it could be concluded that this is not totally surprising given that the main

---

[1] Comparison between *Ageing and Society*, the main UK journal on ageing, and *The Gerontologist*, the USA premier journal, highlights these differences.

waves of immigration to the UK took place in the 1950s and 1970s and consequently ethnic minority populations have a young age profile. In the 2001 census only 6 per cent of non-white ethnic minority groups were over 65, compared to 17 per cent of the white British population (Nazroo, 2006). The ageing of significant numbers of these migrants, particularly Indians and black Caribbeans, has only relatively recently been an issue for care services. The emphasis on the 'youth' of ethnic minority groups, however, has been oversimplified. As Katbamna et al. (2004) point out, this has provided a smokescreen for agencies' lack of response as disability and the need for care has always been present among all age ranges.

The diversity of the care needs of ethnic minorities has not been recognized in previous literature. The tendency was to assume that ethnic minorities 'cared for their own' (Atkin and Rollings, 1993) as much of their care was invisible, and this was exacerbated by service professionals' racist stereotypes (Walker and Ahmad, 1994). A growing number of small-scale qualitative studies looking at patterns of care within ethnic minority groups have exposed and dispelled this and other myths. The analysis of carers' accounts in a study by Bywaters et al. (2003) suggested that, for a variety of reasons, the main carer, irrespective of gender, had limited support in both nuclear and extended households. In more recent research (Sin, 2006; Phillipson et al., 2001) it is clear that Asian Indians, for example, realistically acknowledge that the support that they required was not always available for their children. Blakemore (1997) is also critical of the concentration on the experience of ethnicity relating only to the inner cities, with no literature on rural populations.

Chau and Yu (2000) look at the transitions of twenty Chinese older people from 'double attachment' to 'double detachment'. Chinese communities maintain dual attachment to the host society and to their own community when in paid employment, particularly through the catering trade, and turn to their own community when in need of care and support. Retirement however means a loss of work and attachment to their community. Many were worried about using social services but equally found it difficult to rely on family members and consequently faced social exclusion.

Phillipson et al. (2001) looked at Bangladeshi families in Bethnal Green and found that like the white population women predominantly took on the caring roles, yet they faced extra difficulties in caring for older disabled husbands, often in housing which was overcrowded. Language difficulties were also apparent and hindered their access to formal supports. Communication problems when negotiating with health and social care services were a major issue.

Although the support systems of many ethnic groups, for example Indians, may be strong (Evandrou, 2000) partly through being together in adversity or periods of migration, for others they are weak, for example Bangladeshi women in Tower Hamlets, and are not any more supportive than predominantly white groups. In a study in three areas of England, Asian Indians and Asian Bangladeshis had kin who lived locally yet there were others who were socially isolated and lacked confidence in seeking help from statutory and voluntary agencies (Phillips et al., 2002; Katbamna et al., 2004). More recent research (Butt and Moriarty, 2004) found that carers from South Asian communities did not have support from members of their family and friends outside their household whereas those in black Caribbean families had wide caring networks involving church members and others outside the family.

These studies demonstrated the need for a greater awareness and appreciation of the diversity within and between ethnic minority groups. One of the few studies that compares white British with Asian Indians is a study by Sin (2006). He argues that the interdependence of informal and formal spheres of care is often misunderstood particularly in a cross-cultural context and argues that 'an individual's experience and expectation of one type of support is often made in relation to his or her experience and expectation of other sources of support' (p. 215). His findings demonstrate that Asian Indians have high levels of expectation for support from the family and state compared to white British respondents, who had a high level of expectation for state support regardless of whether they had satisfactory informal social networks.

In many instances patterns of care were similar to those of the white groups, with women predominantly assuming the caring role in multigenerational families. Guberman and Maheu (1999) argue that it is imperative to be sensitive to difference but also to look for similarity in care needs (rejecting the 'assimilation' principle that 'they should be like us'). Blakemore (1997) argues that dependence on 'culturalist' explanations can pathologize minority groups. Similarly accounts which base the issues on class, gender, age and economics without reference to cultural difference can be reductionist.

A further recurring debate in the literature has been about the low take up of services by ethnic minority groups and the lack of appropriate professional response (Ahmad, 1996). Again the diversity across groups is noteworthy.

The negotiation with and appropriateness of health and social services for ethnic minority groups is a recurring theme in the literature, questioning whether services are culturally and ethnically sensitive. A host of studies, again small scale, address these issues to the extent that it is widely held that take up is low because services do not meet the needs of ethnic minority groups and individuals in the UK. Mir and Tovey (2003), who studied the experiences of carers from South Asia caring for a person with cerebral palsy, found that poor communication, limited understanding of the health and social care systems, the stigma felt by the South Asian community and lack of emotional support disadvantaged not only the carer but also the person cared for. Katbamna et al. (2004) published similar findings in relation to South Asian carers. Sin (2006) also finds a lack of awareness of services among Asian Indian groups. Other stereotypes are linked to religious beliefs of minority ethnic groups, which are assumed to be different and to have different cultural associations from those held by the white population (Beresford et al., 1996). Bywaters et al. (2003) found that institutional racism rather than religious attitudes (which were often shared by other groups including the white population) resulted in low level of services to carers of disabled children.

Azmi (1997) emphasizes the need to consider the implications of social diversity for the delivery and provision of social care. In considering a social work case he argues that professionals need to reflect on their own specific ideological viewpoint and recognize the competing welfare ideologies that exist. His research among Muslim communities in Toronto found significant ideological conceptions of welfare and care that were at odds with mainstream Canadian care conceptions. Islamic ideology is embedded within a religious framework and gives primacy to religious identity and beliefs. Welfare activity beyond this boundary is understood as 'missionary in character' (p. 119). In contrast the Canadian system does not divide welfare along religious lines. 'The client is allocated a worker on lines of problem specification and not religious identification' (p. 106).

Professionals defining social diversity do so through a parochial 'cultural' or 'ethnic' lens, which has the effect of hiding cultural variation within minority groups and hence giving rise to perceptions of care that are based on stereotypes (Azmi, 1997). Similarly they may ignore their own ideological viewpoint.

> The idea of secularised and specialized types of care being administered through professional occupational forms is thought to give the contemporary health and social care occupations universal validity. The idea of a transcendent form of care is an alluring notion, but the evidence . . . suggests that it represents a grand illusion. (p. 119)

In the UK context anti-racist social work was promoted through the work of the Central Council for the Education and Training of Social Workers (CCETSW). Naik (1991) writing at the time suggested that social work education attempted to advocate equality for all, promote positive attitudes and diminish prejudice and discrimination as well as permeate the curriculum with a multicultural approach, yet courses still operated within the dominant ideology and white control. A number of years later it could be said that 'cultural competence' among service professionals is inadequate (Acheson, 1998). Yet this is a debatable point which the chapter returns to later.

One of the features of the study by Bywaters et al. (2003) was that low take up resulted even after advocacy services. Begum (2006) looks at why participation of users from black and minority ethnic groups is still low after twenty years of participatory approaches despite there being no evidence to suggest that black and minority ethnic service users do not want to participate. One of the reasons, he concludes, is that policy makers consult with representatives of the black and ethnic minority communities, who may be racist, rather than service users themselves.

> The concepts of citizenship, social inclusion, consumerism, empowerment among others have become the bedrock of public policy and the reform of social 'welfare'. Therefore, there is no substitute for the real lived experience and insight of being a black and minority ethnic person who requires or uses social care resources. Those who work around or represent black and minority ethnic perspectives without direct experience of using social care have a critical part to play in supporting and facilitating the participation of black and minority ethnic service users, but cannot be their authoritative voice. (Begum, 2006, p. 2)

Intersectionality

An increasing literature also focuses around the issue of intersectionality. Many older people, for example, face a 'double or triple jeopardy' of being old and from an ethnic minority group (Norman, 1985) which results in disadvantage in the care system. Nazroo and colleagues (2004), however, conclude in their research on ethnic inequalities in older age groups that claims of multiple hazards are more complex than suggested. Intersectionality, which initially found voice in black feminist writing, has been used by authors (Williams, 1995, 2005) to develop this argument of multiple disadvantages through race, sexuality, gender and class. They argue that these are not just add-ons but contribute equally to their lack of power and authority. Ethnic minorities are significantly disadvantaged and this increases with age. Inequalities within ethnic groups are stark in relation to health (Erens, Primatesta and Prior, 2001) and economic situation (Nazroo, 2003) with Bangladeshi and Pakistani groups faring worse (Nazroo, 2006; Phillipson et al., 2000). Disadvantages are also exaggerated by the locations in which ethnic minorities live – often deprived inner city areas (DETR, 2000). Much of this inequality has stemmed from post-migration experiences with restricted employment opportunities and downturns in the industries and occupations that many migrants were recruited into. Such economic inequalities have translated into health and social care inequalities in later life. Inequalities in the formal response to need have been hidden under the myth that such communities care for their own (see above).

The situation is changing constantly. Older minority populations in the UK are mainly people who migrated to the UK during specific periods of immigration. The next generation of older people are British-born and will have very different attitudes (Nazroo, 2006). In terms of social class, some downward migration has been observed for the second and younger generation groups, particularly Pakistani and Bangladeshi, yet educational attainments are increasing for Bangladeshi girls aged sixteen (White, 2002), suggesting a decrease in the economic inequalities for younger generations. Yet there are other areas, for example in relation to identity, where complexity and inconsistency exist across age and generation.

The inclusion of 1991 and 2001 census data has broadened our understanding of ethnicity and highlighted the considerable diversity in the ethnic backgrounds of minority groups (Nazroo et al., 2004). Such diversity of care within and between ethnic minority groups in the UK has challenged conventional thinking.

Some argue that the term 'diversity' (although often used interchangeably with 'race equality') disguises what has to be challenged and what needs to be achieved in the way that 'anti-racism', 'multiculturalism', 'race equality' among others make explicit (Begum, 2006). Moving away from naming the specific inequalities people encounter to a more integral and diversity-based stance has been seen as a backward step.

Challenges to the theoretical frameworks of care are crucial if we are to understand the concept of care as it applies in the UK today. Comparisons and relations between ethnic groups and between minority and majority groups are essential to our understanding (Blakemore, 1997). Yet there has been relatively little theorizing of care that takes into consideration the diversity of ethnicity, culture and power structures, outside of what has been termed the 'essentialist' discourse of ethnicity. Such a discourse views ethnic groups as static collectives with shared origins and common cultural attributes (Bromley, 1989) and may attribute to them common characteristics to explain their 'difference' from others in relation to their needs and actions of care (hence the 'all minority ethnic groups care for their own' approach). In relation to a caring response from professionals, accessing knowledge of 'other' cultures is seen as the appropriate response – what has been termed a 'fact file' approach.

Whether conceptual frameworks can be transferred across different ethnic groups is a moot point. This becomes even more complex in terms of biculturalism where individuals gain competence in two or more cultures and have cultural identity and ties within both (La Fromboise, Coleman and Gerton, 1993).

This chapter looks at a further argument for an alternative view of theorizing care in minority ethnic cultures and starts by drawing on an article by Culley (2006) in respect of health care. One of her arguments centres on the utility of a postmodern approach in recognizing and embracing diversity and difference. What this chapter illustrates is not only the diversity and complexity of the concept of care but that our starting point and framing of care within our own ethnic and cultural boundary is socially constructed and different from others even within our boundaries.

Multicultural approaches to care

Culley (2006) argues that ethnicity and diversity has been theorized in the caring professions under the banner of transculturalism. Ethnicity rather than racism has been the starting point for people practising care with little recognition that ethnicity is a contested concept. The assumption is that there is a 'common cultural heritage, homogeneity and distinctiveness' (Mulholland, 1995; Culley, 2006). All individuals within particular ethnic groups will act the same based on their cultural and religious norms. 'Culturally sensitive' care can therefore be provided through learning about the differences between such ethnic groups and operationalizing this knowledge at the level of the individual client–worker relationship. Increasingly within this discourse there is recognition of the social context and power relations, yet ethnic groups are seen as 'relatively fixed and uncomplicated cultural groups with defined sets of health beliefs and sets of health behaviours. This apparent contradiction remains largely un-problematised' (p. 148), perpetuating the 'us' and 'them' approach in practice.

'Communicative competence' has been a term used to describe the skills needed to work with ethnic minorities (Gerrish, Husband and Mackenzie, 1996), with an emphasis on more task-oriented learning around behaviour, values and rules of engagement with specific cultural groups. Gunaratnam (1997b) refers to this as a 'fact file' approach where greater cultural knowledge can lead to greater cultural sensitivity and appropriate approaches to care. As she goes on to argue, such knowledge treats culture and race as 'discrete, identifiable conditions. Not unlike medical conditions, that can be observed, categorized and treated/mistreated by practitioners' (p. 122). The dynamics and impact of age, gender, social class and individual biography are ignored in favour of static cultural assumptions.

In rethinking ethnicity, Culley draws on two useful critiques – ethnicity as a social process and the postmodernist view of identity and ethnicity.

Drawing on the work of Barth (1969) she argues that 'ethnicity is about the relationships between groups rather than the content of those groups' (p. 148). Additionally she refers to Nagel's shopping trolley analysis (1994), i.e. the content of culture (the shopping trolley) is not already loaded but is made up of what we choose to put into it. Ethnic identity in this way is therefore changeable. Whereas agency operates at one end, external structural forces also operate at the other in shaping identity and culture. Rather than being static the individual acts within certain cultural norms.

Culley also argues that postmodernism challenges the dominant transcultural perspective.

Individuals are confronted by a multiplicity of possible identities based on a number of differences – gender, age, class,
religion and ethnicity, which may be more or less important
in different contexts. Identifications are contextual. This
undermines the stable conceptual categories commonly used
in the idea of culturally sensitive care. (p. 150)

In taking the argument further she finds Bourdieu's notion
of habitus (1990) and May's (1999) translation of this as
critical 'multiculturalism' are important concepts in relation
to (health) care. The essentials of these two concepts offer a
reflexive position, acknowledging power differentials and
diversity in space as well as time, as cultures reconstruct
themselves in response to outside influences, and take ethnicity beyond its bounded dimensions.

Whereas transcultural notions have offered professionals
security, ways of knowing and a set of tasks (Gunaratnam,
1997b), multiculturalism can be uncomfortable and uncertain depending on changing contexts. It can be argued that
practice has sheltered under the former approach with its
emphasis on competency-based, task-focused practice, particularly in social care. Theorizing care under a critical multicultural banner can be liberating for practice and can
promote care 'across cultural boundaries' as well as person-
centred care without taking a racist approach. Defining
people solely in terms of their ethnicity without considering
the wider power differentials and the complexities of the
changing nature of ethnicity can be detrimental to practice
and miss the differences within groups as well as between
groups, an argument which parallels the notion of intersectionality discussed earlier. For example, not all Asians are
Muslims and have certain practices in relation to care.

Issues of race, culture and care have no political boundaries. Debates on multiculturalism are echoed in many societies
and the debate has global implications. Ehrenreich and
Hoschild (2002) talk of the 'global care chain' where poor
women from the southern hemisphere care for wealthy
northern hemisphere children leaving their own children and
older relatives back home to be cared for by others. The
power differential expands as their relationship to each other
is as employer–employee, mistress and maid. Across the

world there are changes in the way families operate vis-à-vis the state and political, social and economic changes are all impacting on family care even in states traditionally recognized as family-based systems such as those based on Confucianism and where filial piety (devotion, obedience and care towards one's parents and elderly family members) operates, such as China and Japan. Mehta and Thang (forthcoming) discuss this conceptual change in Singapore with the introduction of the domestic maid, carrying out tasks from household chores and child minding to care for older parents. Intergenerational interdependence is being challenged by the economic necessity of women's role in the workplace and this in turn is challenging the commonly held view of filial piety. The Singapore government's encouragement of 'an extra pair of hands' through policies to promote domestic maids, however, is an attempt to save face on filial piety.

> It is a paradox that the hiring of a maid facilitates the continuity of filial responsibility on the part of the adult children, yet it could blur the boundaries between direct filial care from adult child and purchased care delivered in the family home, albeit paid for by the adult child. In the eyes of the society, as long as the elder person is kept within the family fold, his/her co-resident adult child is being filial, even though the major part of physical (and even emotional) care is being provided by the foreign maid . . . As long as the stigma attached to institutionalization continues, the foreign maid as an eldercare assistant would be a viable and desired option for the Singaporean families that can afford to have one. (Mehta and Thang, forthcoming)

The blurring is not only between paid and unpaid, private and public, but also between locales of care. It is the blurring that Mehta and Thang refer to that is changing and challenging all conceptualizations of care, particularly in the global world where care is interconnected. In Phillipson et al.'s (2001) study, care for ethnic minority elders was shared in a number of ways across continents. Inter-country adoption is also becoming a significant issue. It is this theme of globalization and care which is picked up in chapter 7.

Despite there being a concentration on small-scale descriptive studies of ethnic minority groups in the care literature in the UK, such studies provide the building blocks of any conceptualization. The debates discussed in this chapter heighten the need to look at cross-group issues around care both within the UK and beyond. Studies exposing myths and highlighting inequalities will provide a better basis for policy and practice as well as enable a reframing of care within a global conceptualization.

7
The Geography of Care

In chapter 6 the concept of care was explored in relation to its cultural context, yet such cultural notions of care cannot be divorced from their geographical rootedness. Moving on from who provides care, this chapter addresses the spatial context of care – the issue of where care is provided. Understanding the meaning and importance of different locations of care is central to how people conduct and analyse their caring role yet geography is often invisible in the care literature. The location in which care is performed and negotiated can be stigmatized (for example in the institution), stereotyped (the retirement community) or sentimentalized (as with home). All these images may reflect myth rather than reality but have important consequences in how care relationships are played out.

The chapter addresses spaces and places of care. Space is seen as an abstract, multiple and plural concept whereas place is space transformed and given cultural meaning by human activity (Cartier, 2003). Place not only provides a location for caregiving but can be a site where complex social relationships are played out in relation to other spheres of life: work, home and wider social relationships (Massey, 1994).

The environment is shaped and conditioned by those you live with as well as the physical space in which these relations develop (Fry, 2003). Spaces and places are also tied to meanings and memories (Peace, Holland and Kellaher, 2006; Rowles, 1978), attachments (Scharf et al., 2002) and identities (Peace et al., 2006). Taking a spatial perspective on the social dynamics of care across the lifecourse is therefore important. Both space and place are seen as important concepts, being linked with well-being and ageing well, where well-being is defined as achieving a 'person-environment fit' (Lawton and Nahemow, 1973; McPherson, 2004). Time as well as space is important in this context. As families and individuals move through the lifecourse the need for more or less space may mean a change of location; similarly when care is needed a 'lack of fit' or inappropriateness of the physical environment may require a change of place and readjustment of space (Lawton, 1980). This assumes that people have 'agency' in relation to their environments and can mould and shape them to suit their needs; this, however, may not be possible in relation to some people in need of care.

This chapter addresses the following debates in looking at the geography of care:

1. Location – where and under what circumstances is the ideal location for care? The jury firmly ruled in the 1970s that the familiarity of 'home' was the preferred option over the institution. This appears to hold as a precious notion throughout the lifecourse. What is important about the notion and meaning of 'home'? Similarly there are stereotypes of care in rural and urban locations – is it best to grow old in an urban or rural environment when care is required?
2. The interconnection between the social and the spatial is highlighted by looking at distance and proximity. The debate is increasingly being focused on migration and the globalization of care and the distances people travel to negotiate care and to act as caregivers. Globalization has transformed our notions and perceptions of space and place and questioned the nature and extent of care provision. How does distance impact on care?

Underpinning all these aspects is the issue of time – lifecourse and generational time will both impact on care locations.

This chapter will examine and evaluate locations of care at different stages of the lifecourse. How does the location of care change as we move through the lifecourse? Finally the chapter discusses a reconceptualization of care using a caringscapes perspective; a multidimensional approach to care rather than boundarying it within particular stereotyped locales as discussed in chapter 5.

> Caringscapes can be thought of as shifting and changing multi-dimensional terrain that comprises people's vision of caring responsibilities and obligations: routes that are influenced by everyday scheduling. People create routes through caringscapes which change and evolve as they move through the lifecourse. (McKie et al., 2004, p. 2)

Location of care

There are a number of levels on which care can be positioned. Traditionally the debates on location and caregiving have focused on the advantages of 'home' and disadvantages of 'institutional' care. This dichotomy is applied throughout the lifecourse, whether it is in relation to child care (adoption and fostering over residential care) or care in later life (living independently for as long as possible at home rather than entering a care home). These divisions are simplistic as there are many forms of institutional care, ranging from a community home with education to retirement communities with a heavy emphasis on communal care.

Residential versus home care

Following the work of Goffman (*Asylums*, 1961), Townsend (*The Last Refuge*, 1962), Miller and Gwynne (*A Life Apart*, 1972), and a host of other studies demonstrating the negative effects of institutional care on people's lives, de-institutionalization became a political goal. Common themes in these studies included: depersonalization and batch living; institutionalization, where residents or patients accept the loss of self and the power of the institution; a lack of choice, autonomy, dignity and privacy; lack of purpose (horticultural, maintenance, warehousing); poor quality staffing and resourcing; and poor transitions to care. The following extract from *The Last Refuge* painted a historic but powerful picture:

> Ainsley House was built in the 1880s . . . and opened as a home in 1956. . . . There is no lift though 50 of the 64 beds are on the first floor, mostly in rooms for 3, 4, 5 or 6 people. . . . I noticed that the rooms were usually bare of personal possessions, though as in other Homes where furnishings are few, clothes were occasionally to be seen hanging at the ends of the beds. . . . some of the rooms are extremely dark. The lino in a few of the w.c.s is saturated with urine and in two there were leaves of a telephone directory and not toilet paper. (Townsend, 1962, p. 114)

Milligan (2003), drawing on the work of Augé, argues that such places are still characterized by anonymity and represent non-spaces, lacking anthropological meaning.

Institutions have come to be seen as inherently undesirable. Alternatively, community care increasingly continues to be seen as 'good' spaces for care. Community care was promoted as best care throughout 1970s and 1980s and this was embodied in a series of government documents, white papers and in legislation (*A Happier Old Age*, 1978; *Growing Older*, 1981 and the NHS and Community Care Act 1990). Institutional living however could not be ignored and came into focus during the explosion of private residential care provision. New forms of residential care developed in the 1980s within the private sector when care was marketed through smaller 'domestic' family-run settings. Despite the domesticity of such enterprises, the attitude of staff and design of such environments was still important in influencing the quality of care residents received and the degree to which they could maintain personal control (Peace, Kellaher and Willcocks, 1997). The independent sector now dominates the residential and nursing care market and provides diverse images of care. The larger corporate sector has now entered the business, with larger 'places' of care being established; few domestic-type homes remain (Laing and Buisson, 2003).

While the micro environment of care is important we also need to be aware of the macro environment. Institutions consume large amounts of government money and cannot be ignored as locations of care. The quality of care is also a government concern covered through a range of regulations and standards which residential and nursing homes have to follow (through the Care Standards Act 2000). The stringent application of standards has, however, led to home closures with home size and occupancy significantly associated with the probability of a home closing (Darton, 2004). Debates within the care arena are now focusing more on the issue of quality of life and quality of care rather than the dichotomy between home and institutional life (Help the Aged, 2006).

The location of care within and outside of institutions has also been an area of continuing debate in relation to children in need. Bowlby's work and findings of the Tavistock Institute (1951–80) in relation to maternal bonding strongly emphasized the location of 'home' as the ideal environment to raise children. Long-term placement with family and friends is more successful than other forms of long-term placement, such as institutions (Butler, 2000). By 2000 only 12 per cent of 'looked after' children were in residential homes; a percentage that had declined over the 1980s and 1990s. It is generally children with behavioural or offending problems that are accommodated in this way. For those in residential care there is still a notion of parents retaining responsibility under the Children Act 1989 with an effort directed at maintaining links and contact with birth parents (Corby, 2000). Research on children leaving care after 16 years of age also highlights the detrimental effects that institutional life can have on children (Ward, 1995). This includes being unprepared for life particularly in relation to further education, work and independence.

Whereas institutions are seen as 'placeless', home is seen as the ideal. This is not surprising as the meaning of home is an increasingly important theme in the discussion of our identity, control, privacy, security, safety, permanency, independence, freedom, individuality and autonomy (Peace, Holland and Kellaher, 2006; Sixsmith, 1986). Individual biography and personal history are linked to home and it is an inseparable part of ourselves where we act out fantasy and fiction, express ourselves and create our identities. As we travel through the lifecourse, objects within a home take on significant meanings (Rowles, 2005). Individualization means we are spending longer on our own at home. Familiarity and territoriality are important in the provision of care.

However it could be argued that there is an overrating of home as some home environments are unsuitable in design or hold bad memories, and people can be imprisoned in their home and locality through poverty and poor design (Phillips et al., 2005). People may face 'forced independence' through stereotyped and romanticized notions of home. Some would argue that 'ageing in place' is becoming more like institutional living (Milligan, 2006). Institutionalization can also occur in the community because of isolation and immobility (Victor et al., 2005; Women's Royal Volunteer Service, 2004; McCarthy and Thomas, 2004). Barclay as far back as 1982 cautioned against the tsunami of opinion on home at all costs. Children too are not immune from family abuse in the home as chapter 9 explores.

'Private' space is also becoming contested ground with the increasing emphasis on community care and the provision of formal care in the home. Milligan (2003) argues that such spaces are becoming non-places, similar to institutional spaces where transience and movement occur and where home becomes a place of work for professionals and care workers. The boundaries between professional and personal spaces are becoming blurred (Martin-Matthews and Mahmood, forthcoming).

In relation to caregiving, interconnecting the social and the spatial can be both liberating and constraining. Locking women into the private spatial sphere of the home can limit their identity to that of carers. Caregivers are restricted spatially and with the focus of their care 'at home' they are constructed as being oriented to certain values with regard to obligation and duty (Wiles, 2003). As Martin-Matthews (2007) illustrates in her paper 'Situating "home" at the nexus of the public and private spheres', this can extend to paid care workers in the space of 'home' as well as family carers. Renegotiating identities and activities in relation to place will occur as care roles change (Wiles, 2003).

Urban, rural or suburban: where is the best location for care?

Community care has been viewed with rose-coloured spectacles in many contexts. The debate around the friendliness and supportive nature of rural communities is one such myth. Contradictions exist in relation to the rural context of ageing: that they are environments where distance leads to isolation but alternatively are rich in people resources where older adults are embedded in strong networks of family and friends (Keating and Phillips, forthcoming). One of the factors ignored in the simplistic debate is the diversity of all environments. Whether rural or urban there is difference within these contexts – no one rural place is like another. Living in the remote regions of Northern Canada, for example, will be different from living in a rural village in the south of England in terms of perceptions of distance, access to care facilities and the way in which they are delivered, shopping facilities and work environment, let alone topography and climate. The stereotype of rural older people having a network of neighbours, friends and family nearby to provide support may indeed exist but when it comes to providing care it is evident that the network can shrink (Tennstedt, McKinlay and Sullivan, 1989) or be diverse in their support (Wenger and Keating, forthcoming). Wenger and Keating (forthcoming) provide evidence of the diversity of support and care networks over time in a typology of rural care networks. Drawing on data from the Bangor Longitudinal Study of Ageing, conducted over twenty years in rural Wales, they found that care networks were most likely to emerge from *family dependent* and *locally integrated* support network types yet the core of the care network was in almost all cases a daughter or other close female relative. *Wider community focused* support networks evolved into care networks only if there is a spouse present. *Local self-contained* and *privately restricted* support networks did not develop into care networks and reliance on formal care services was common.

Care in rural areas will have different dimensions. Providing support with transport to the nearest facilities is different from providing personal care, which is often seen as the domain of the family. Yet family of a younger generation may have chosen to leave the community in search of work in the nearest cities. There are also gender dimensions: older women are more likely to have larger network support than men across countries and ethnic groups (Kim et al., 2000) as women are seen to be the 'kin keepers' and 'confidants' (Phillipson et al., 2001). They are also likely to be providing the care to others. In a study of farming families in Northern Ireland, Heenan (2000) explored the concept of carer and found that women in such communities found the concept meaningless and irrelevant; they took pride in looking after their families and ignored formal services. Cultural rules and assumptions built up across generations around the 'farming family' governed the care arena. It is interesting, however, to note that in the Canadian context in remote areas with resources, for example mining towns where men come into the community to work, it is men who are engaged in support networks as women, particularly after the death of a husband, will leave for larger service centres (Joseph and Martin-Matthews, 1993).

Increasingly populations are becoming more suburban and this can result in particular issues in relation to care that perhaps mirror stereotypes of both urban and rural, for example difficulties with transport and access to facilities. There is a need therefore to question the continuing polarity between home and institution, urban and rural as bases for studying care. Place may not be the overriding factor in respect of the provision of care and support – it may depend on how connected people are to each other.

However on the macro level of policy environment, place may be a significant factor. Across the UK there are inequalities in terms of access to care, different eligibility criteria

Case study

Alice lives in the Scottish Highlands. She had poliomyelitis as a child which has left her very disabled. She has been receiving treatment for lung cancer which has meant regular travelling to the nearest hospital twenty miles away. She relies on neighbours to drive her to the city three times a week but due to her disability has to wake at 5.30 am to make an 11 am appointment. There are no local pharmacies or day care and consequently Alice has to spend longer in intermediate care in the city than is usual. For those working in this environment, such as nurses and social workers, it is important to understand the context in which Alice lives and the impact of distance on her care and recovery. For Alice intermediate care provides her with more independence than she enjoys at home. Specialist technology enables her to shop locally without relying on staff or friends. She is able to eat regularly as staff members prepare her meals and she can conveniently exercise in the swimming pool. Although this is a temporary move Alice has started to think of her future care and the best place to secure regular quality care and an environment that is supportive to her needs.

(regarding hospital discharge or rehabilitation), different charges and different systems and structures of care (Tudor Hart, 1971).

Distance and proximity of care

Distance is an important factor in the care literature. Contact and care are intertwined, particularly when personal hands-on care is required. Most studies look at residential proximity in terms of children living with older parent(s) or those who can provide daily care because of living within a ten- to twenty-minute journey. Geographical proximity was considered a necessary requirement in the provision of care (Aldous and Klein, 1991), denying the possibility of long-distance care. This can still be true of care for children, as most children live with their parents or guardians and care provision is within the household as opposed to from outside the household as is the case in adult and particularly parent care. Early studies on caregiving in the context of family life focused on contact and care and looked at residential proximity. The classic British studies on the family life of older people (Townsend, 1957; Young and Willmott, 1957; Sheldon, 1948) showed how proximity played a crucial part in the provision of care, both emotionally and practically. In these studies, households containing older people were often complex and multigenerational. Intergenerational reciprocity of care occurred on a daily basis and older people were surrounded by others with whom they had close and supportive relationships – both within and beyond their own households. They lived essentially within what Frankenburg (1966) termed 'an environment of kin' and the more intimate the care, the more bounded were the places and spaces in which that care was transacted. These studies also showed that the heaviest care fell to those who were co-resident or living nearby.

In today's generation, where cross-national and even international migration is commonplace, caring at a distance has become an important issue for many families faced with caring responsibilities. Migration and globalization have opened up the possibility of care spanning different continents and led to a reconceptualization of distance care based on the complex interconnections between individuals who live at great distances. Distance from the care recipient influences the decision about who becomes the primary carer, and it can be argued that caring at a distance should be considered to be a distinct form of caring faced with some difficulties dissimilar to those in other care situations.

Perceptions of time and space, along with mode of transport, and personal-time budgets will influence distance. Mason (1999) describes as 'distance thinkers' people who reason that it is possible to conduct kin relations at a distance, seeing geographical distance as compatible with the development of meaningful relationships or as Rosenmayr and Köckeis (1963) call it 'intimacy at a distance'. The nature of the environments in which people live and work also means that it might often take a fairly long time to travel even short distances.

With greater geographical dispersion being more of a feature of family life, children (as well as other relatives) are now much more likely to maintain separate households than they did forty years or more ago. Indeed, the study by Phillipson et al. (2001) of the family life of older people conducted in the same geographical areas as those of Townsend (1957), Young and Willmott (1957) and Sheldon (1948) found that older people today have, at most, only one child close by (within four miles). People are also commuting long distances to work (Green, Hogarth and Shackleton, 1999) which again will affect their ability to provide care on a daily basis. However, longer distances of necessity tend to change the kind of care that can be offered. In one sense then, distance very much imposes boundaries on care – at least on the practical and intimate tasks that might need to be performed. On the other hand, distance has become blurred and compressed by the advent of modern technologies which enable emotional, if not practical, support to be given in ways not accessible to previous generations of carers.

The provision of 'hands-on' care clearly remains a task constrained by distance and research has consistently found that distance thresholds operate (Neal et al., 2003; Phillips, Bernard and Chittenden, 2002a). Phillips et al. (2002) found far fewer carers providing care at distances over thirty minutes' travelling time away. Ley and Waters (2004) have argued that a 'spatial stickiness' operates as a consequence of the physical separation. They discuss this in relation to what they term 'astronaut' families. These are family members who relocate their families to Vancouver yet conduct their business from Taiwan and commute between the two locations. This in turn has fundamental implications for family relationships as older members transported to Canada may be left isolated and away from their 'home'. They suggest that there is a geographical imperative continuing to reward spatial proximity over separation when it comes to family care and the sustainability of relationships.

Case study

Indira Sagal lives in London, while her elderly mother remains in India with her extended family. Indira sends money back home to provide care for her mother and visits frequently. In emergencies she is regularly called back to India as she is 'the only one my mother trusts'. Increasingly she finds this is causing difficulty with her employer and recently a social worker has become involved as life is becoming more difficult and Indira has been experiencing severe anxiety. As part of reorganizing her life she is considering moving her mother to England. In talking through the issues with Indira the social worker will need to explore the cultural dimensions of a move as well as the physical and psychological changes that may result. Language will be an issue for her mother as well as the social care staff in the residential home, some of whom will also have English as their second language.

Parker, Call and Kosberg (2001) found that distance has a substantial negative impact on personal contact with parents, particularly for distances greater than 100 miles. Personal visits are largely determined by distance whereas telephone calls result from the nature of the relationship with parents and the health condition of parents. Living in a different country also has widely ranging different constraints and expectations for care and contact.

The inability to visit regularly may create conflict and guilt for some carers (Baldock, 2000). They may be forced to cope with anxiety and stress through telephone and email contact. Connidis (2001) in her work found that ambivalence in relationships can also be created through distance. As distance increases, substitution of contact types occurs (Dewit, Wister and Burch, 1988; Keeling, 2001) with friends taking the place of family (Keeling, 2001).

Distance can also be seen in a positive as well as a negative light. 'Legitimate distance' (Campbell and Martin-Mathews, 2003) means that greater distance may be a legitimate reason for less care involvement and can lead to more regular emotional support through the telephone.

As chapter 5 highlighted, our sense of space and place is gendered and care spaces are generally the domain of women.

Women tend to take on the primary carer role yet the literature on distance appears contradictory with one report finding that men provide more long-distance care than women (Wagner, 2003). As samples were chosen from corporations and workplaces then this may not be surprising. However earlier literature suggested that it was women who travelled longer distances to provide more intimate care (Joseph and Hallman, 1996).

In one Canadian study, men who live closer to their relatives are more likely to provide care than men who live at a distance (Campbell, 2000). Neal et al. (2003) in looking at the effects of distance on long-distance working 'sandwich' generation couples found that more men than women provide the 'most' care to a parent-in-law; husbands are drawn into the wife's family; distance has more significant and negative effects on men (except for wives caring for parents-in-law), a similar finding to that of Wagner (2003).

Distance and care also can take on other dimensions. An increasing issue in the literature revolves around the growing numbers of retired migrants from the UK to the Mediterranean (King, Warnes and Williams, 2000). As migrants who do not wish to return to the UK are reaching older ages and have increased heath and social care needs there is a need for local responses. In some cases they are no longer the responsibility of the UK and are not fully recognized in their new country (Hardill et al., 2005). Whereas social capital is restricted for some through migration, for others such changes can lead to new ways of relating. In relation to South Asians, Mand (2006) argues that 'migration is a household decision and is related to the needs of members. At the same time, migration influences the ways in which family life is experienced and how members relate to one another. . . . Correspondingly, these new forms of social relatedness to people and places are enacted through practices involving rituals, and care and provision' (p. 9).

The impact of distance on work

One of the main questions on the work–life balance agenda has been the impact of caregiving on work. The job effects of elder care will differ depending on whether the caregiver lives with the care recipient or lives some distance away. Distance is predictive of difficulties in balancing work and care (Wagner, 2003) yet caregiver stress may not increase with increasing distance (Kolb, 2003). If the distance is very great, this can have severe impact on work as days and even weeks (for international travel) may have to be taken off work.

Joseph and Hallman (1996) investigate the 'locational triangle', in other words the spatial arrangement between the employed caregiver's home, their workplace and the care recipient's home. They found that stress and interference with work resulted from the spatial arrangements of home, work and older relative. 'Travel time to work impinged on the work side of work-family balance while travel time to older person [impinged] on the family side' (p. 408). Family interference with work was greater for those with dual responsibilities. In terms of adjustment the home–elder care axis was the domain most affected by distance as it, and not the care–work axis, had to be altered to accommodate both functions.

Although there is limited evidence to suggest that being a manager impacts unevenly on care, socio-economic status does have an impact – the higher the education the greater the geographic distance between parents and children (Lin and Rogerson, 1995), but higher income may mean more money for travel. Visiting relatives over long distances is not without cost.

Time and place

Families have a geography as well as a history over time; over the lifecourse they may change in relation to space and place. Care and caring are closely related to lifecourse time: 'we give care to others and receive care from others at particular life course phases. . . . Care raises issues concerning generational time: the reciprocities that take place between family members, across time and at any one moment in time' (Brannen, 2002).

The suitability of locations and environments for care will also change across the lifecourse. As families expand, the need for increasing space may lead to a change in location and similarly when family members are in need of care the inappropriateness or 'lack of fit' of the physical environment may require a change in place and readjustment of space (Lawton, 1980).

Location and care therefore require a lifecourse perspective. Earlier events in the lifecourse will have an impact, for example having children. Different periods in the lifecourse may require relocation depending on the individual's circumstances. McKie et al. (2004) describe such transitions as 'caringscapes' – time–space frameworks, in which care is carried out through the lifecourse. Planned caring routes can be altered in response to certain events such as the birth of a child or declining health of an older person. Caringscapes engage with activities, feelings and reflective positions in people's mapping and shaping of routes through caring. This reflects some of the notions of Hagerstrand's time–space geography of the 1970s where place and space are constrained by time and distance. A caringscapes perspective offers a more flexible and less deterministic view of caring and space.

Warnes (1992) and Wagner (2002) also look at the family caregiving trajectory and adjustments that carers make to accommodate older members. Accommodations may be to defy or deny distance (Phillips et al., 2002) and can include a long commute; relying on other more proximate family members to provide support; relocating to be nearer the parent; relocating a parent to a child's home; or moving the parent to residential care nearer the child.

In viewing the literature on place, space and care through a spatial lens there are a number of debates which have challenged our geographically specific stereotypes. Home may not be the ideal place for care at various points in the lifecourse. Home can also exist in a residential setting. Are we therefore stigmatizing and damaging an important location of care by associating it with an outmoded image of institutional life? Are our visions of care leading to age, gender and ethnic segregation? New forms of care that combine community living and home are emerging through retirement communities; technology and care through smart homes are broadening our concepts of place and care and providing us with a more holistic view. Care is not about looking after or being dependent, it encompasses the whole of life. We need therefore a more flexible way of viewing care locations that encompasses both spatial and social relationships, as it is not environment alone that defines care but the connectedness between people within the environment. In reconceptualizing care we need to take a caringscapes approach, moving us from the 'best' places for care to a more flexible notion of change to meet care needs, one which challenges the dominant power inherent in particular spaces.

In such a reconceptualization for Indira, who featured in the second case study in this chapter, care at a distance might be sustained if support systems were in place in both places. In assessment it is vital that professionals in health and social care do not jump to conclusions about the impossible nature of care across distances. For Alice taking a caringscapes approach would mean assessing the appropriateness of the environmental context in relation to her lifecourse and attachments.

On a macro level there are wider planning issues. Part of this debate is where to physically site facilities of care and how the siting impacts on choice of home for potential residents and carers. This goes along with perceptions and discrimination as people protest 'not in my backyard'. Connecting spaces and places is also of importance as transport issues can mediate care relations, and environmental design and architecture will also have an impact on places of care.

8
Professional Debates Surrounding Care

So far this book has addressed key definitional and theoretical concepts and ideas centring on the notion of social care in its broadest sense. The application of the concept of care and the way in which it is received by different groups of people, for example, those from ethnic minorities, older people and women, has been touched upon. The debate in this chapter moves into the professional arena where in many instances the power over the decisions related to care is located.

The translation of ideas into practice throws up a number of dilemmas and debates for professionals which are philosophical, ethical, political and practical in nature. Previous chapters discussed the complexity of care, and the difficulties in ring-fencing and defining care. In this chapter we address the professionalization of care where care is routinely defined within boundaries by different organizations and academic interests and is tied in with need, access, eligibility criteria and managerial considerations as well as ethics, values, philosophies and principles.

Whereas chapter 3 looked at how care policy has been dictated by ideological and political change, care has also been shaped by changes in social science theory and professional opinion. Examples of such are evident both in early years – for example Bowlby's early 1950s theories of maternal deprivation and attachment stressed the importance of care in the first five years of life – and later in life, for example Wolfensberger's (1980) principle of normalization and valorization applied to people with a learning disability. Both evidence-based approaches have influenced the way and the context in which intervention and care is delivered.

Paradigms of care have also shifted with professional and local authority organizational influence. Child care has moved to an emphasis on child protection; mental health care to one of a paradigm of risk; learning disability to one of normalization and integration; care of offenders to a paradigm of justice rather than welfare; and for older people care has shifted to person-centred approaches (for example, the National Service Framework for Older People) with an emphasis on independence. A generic notion of care has been superseded by specialization depending on the client or user group under consideration. Much of this change has come with changing political ideologies and an aversion to risk taking in organizations. The boundaries of care can therefore be set by professional and academic expertise as well as the need for organizations to cover themselves from being held responsible. Power is also vested in professionals to define access to care, through the criterion of 'suitability'.

Care is also well defined in relation to 'suitability to care'. One example can be found in foster care. Suitability to care includes material provision as well as emotional support. Care standards agencies also set a definition of care through defining the quality of care that can be expected at home and in institutions. There is also a prescription of care within the criminal justice system regarding how suspects are interviewed, for example the requirement that an 'appropriate adult' be present when young offenders are interviewed. The planning of nursing care prescribes tasks which are considered as care.

Despite such emphases on care there is an argument that such boundarying has led to a de-professionalization of care. Many organizations and professions have been criticized for a mechanistic and fragmented approach to care and, indeed, an impersonal lack of care. Two examples highlight this approach: a care management system introduced into the social services in the UK in early 1990s, and the operation of the health and social care systems resulting in difficulties in the integration of health and social care.

Professional dilemmas around boundaries also operate at a more local level in relation to carework between carers in the 'formal' sector caught between their organizational roles and their commitment to their service user group; this will be highlighted in this chapter. Part of this dilemma is rooted in the fact that it is easier to define the tasks performed by staff than the emotional labour they provide. Additionally managers have become distanced from the coal face of practice and their priorities diverge from those of carers working with older people, children and other vulnerable adults. There may be conflict therefore between the best interests of individuals and the needs of the organization.

Care management

Screening, assessment, care planning, implementation and then monitoring and review of care need are all components of the process of care management. Within social work in particular the emphasis has been on the management of this cycle of care rather than on the direct provision of services, including a qualified social work service. Challis (1999), in his analysis of care management, highlighted the core skills involved: well developed skills in listening and interpersonal relations, collaborative working, communication, thinking outside the professional box, understanding of needs, awareness of local resources, assessment skills, and ability to work across a range of agencies, yet such skills have been eroded. Research by Weinberg et al. (2003) found that care managers spent 64 per cent of their working week in direct and indirect user- and carer-related activities and 32 per cent of their time on administration. This did not differ from the pattern prior to NHS and community care reforms. However, the way managers use the time spent with users and carers has shifted to a more bureaucratic assessment with an emphasis on documentation rather than counselling and supportive work. Such changes have led some commentators to conclude that the care arena has been dumbed down, moving from a professional service to one where unqualified workers operate unsupervised according to a set of mechanistic rules, leading to unsatisfactory outcomes both for service users and for professionals (Henwood, 1995; Richards, 2000). Social work in particular has suffered. The key question remains: to what extent can practices such as care management incorporate principles and an ethic of care as described earlier in this book?

The UK adopted an administrative and bureaucratic care management practice following its success in the US as a way of enabling and ensuring the coordination of services. Its widespread adoption was enshrined in the NHS and Community Care Act of 1990. In the UK this had followed a limited and well funded set of demonstration products carried out by the Personal Social Services Research Unit (PSSRU) (Challis and Davies, 1986) with qualified social workers with low caseloads. Its applicability to the whole of the country's social services and social care users was always questionable. It can be argued that with generous funding and ample provision of professional staff many different paradigms of practice would also demonstrate good practice and positive outcomes. One of the enduring criticisms of the approach has been the resource-driven nature of care management with the emphasis on meeting needs as quickly as possible. With large caseloads and resource limitations a concentration on the interpersonal elements surrounding care has been lost.

In 2003 the Social Services Inspectorate (SSI) commented:

> Like our previous reports we have identified significant, continuing shortfalls in the efficient operation of care management. In many councils this undermined the delivery of good outcomes for users, jeopardised staff morale, and reflected organisational inefficiencies. (p. 5)
>
> In most councils care management was not fully effective and systems needed improvement. Bureaucratic processes and a lack of adequate IT support undermined many councils' efforts. In councils inspected care plans were mostly basic or unsatisfactory. Improved care plans are a key feature in preventing users from experiencing delays. (p. 33)

Care management appears to be inconsistent with the key essentials of an ethic of care. Care is part of a relationship, which includes relationships with professionals as well as informal carers. Within care management the relationship elements of care do not feature centre stage in the service to be delivered. Care is no longer seen as integral to the relationship with a care manager or social worker.

Further, it can be argued that such a resource-driven system fails to see caring as a moral obligation guiding human agency. A stark consideration of this has been the radical overhaul of the probation service from its roots in a Christian tradition of police court missionaries. Formerly guided by moral principle, it has now been translated into a service which relies heavily on targets, resources and rates of reoffending, together with a service based on competition in the private market of security. Previously an agency dedicated to 'advising, assisting and befriending' as a route to rehabilitation, it is now required to visibly provide punishment and management of risk. Difference and diversity is often not taken into account, despite a focus on individual needs-led assessment; standardized services and assessment based on different criteria operate.

Case study

Jennifer is a 26-year-old person with a learning disability. She has been referred to her GP following anxiety attacks and challenging behaviour at the day care centre. Social care workers have put this down to her learning disability but the social worker called in to assess her takes a holistic view of the situation, discovering that it is a problem between her parents that is at the root of her anxiety. This can only be ascertained after several interviews with the social worker.

Collective action and citizenship are not the bases on which care management exists. A right to care is not a guiding principle and the 'collectivist traditions' of carework have been downplayed with the emphasis on the individual rather than on collective action and community development. The system creates dependency rather than interdependence – a key feature of citizenship. Choice is also not an option.

A further area for professional debate is the lack of integration between health and social care.

The integration of health and social care

So far in this book we have concentrated on social aspects of care. Health care is often difficult to disentangle from social care, for example in relation to bathing (Twigg, 2001). The strengthening of professions has reinforced the division between the two arenas and clashes with the policy impetus for integration and partnership. The relationship is further complicated by health care being located within the National Health Service while social care lies within the scope of the local authorities.

Care is a holistic concept not just limited to the health and social aspects of people's lives yet often in policy and practice terms care is boundaried in artificial and unimaginative ways. Talking about health, social care and housing in a holistic fashion is only a relatively recent development, with the actual practice of integration lagging behind and in many areas non-existent. Even in countries of the UK such as Wales and Northern Ireland where there are coterminous organizational structures in place to facilitate this, there is evidence that working together to provide seamless care has still not been achieved.

The medical-social boundary is particularly contentious in relation to the location of personal care. Twigg in a classic article in 1997 'Deconstructing the "Social Bath": help with bathing at home for older and disabled people' in the *Journal of Social Policy,* explores this in relation to the 'social bath', that is the bath that community nursing services would not provide, determining it to be a social bath. The vacuum of responsibility in providing a bath highlighted the differences between the medical and the social. 'The medical and the social exist in an asymmetrical relationship in which the medical is the marked category and the social the unmarked, residual one; . . . the medical gaze constitutes and defines the field; and the medical is legitimised and the social optional' (Twigg, 1997).

Such divisions have been a key issue particularly in terms of who should foot the bill for long-term care, the state or the individual, and what should fall under the remit of health or social services. The character of long-term care gives it an ambiguous position in the care system as it involves health and social elements of care.

Part of long-term care is personal care, which is 'Care that directly involves touching a person's body (and therefore incorporates issues of intimacy, personal dignity and confidentiality) and is distinct both from treatment and therapy and from indirect care such as home help' (Sutherland Report, 1999, p. 67). Personal care is not straightforward. It lies on the fault line of community care that divides the two territories of health and social care yet there is no single definition of the boundary. Boundaries overlap and have become increasingly blurred over the last decade.

The division has both a professional and a knowledge base. Health care professionals look to medicine for their authority and knowledge base. Social care activities fall under the remit of social work. Most workers in this sector have no formal qualifications, but their practice is shaped by social work values (subject to change through managerial approaches) and social work is a less strong profession. Table 8.1 highlights the differences between the medical and social approaches.

The clash of professions has most recently appeared in the debates surrounding 'bed blocking' and discharge of older people from hospital. The reality of this boundarying of care has been amply demonstrated by the problems

Table 8.1 Medical-social distinctions in care

	Cure	Care
Condition	Acute	Chronic
Status	High	Low
Setting	Hospital	Home/community
Profession	Doctor, male	Nurse, female
Care principles	Rationality	Emotion, intuition
Funding per contract	High	Low

surrounding discharge, which have had significant impact on older people. They include:

- Institutional structures and professional boundaries with the history of the social worker as the doctor's 'hand-maiden'. Power relationships within hospital can define whether a need is social or medical.
- Professional background: difficulties in deciding who is responsible for what, discharge nurse or social worker for example.
- Lack of recognition of a social work role by patients/ service users: no sense that their care was being 'managed'. Carers similarly felt ill informed.
- Professional rivalry and other workers' ignorance of the care management role: conflicting views of the social role.
- Bed blocking as a political hot potato: reports that people discharged 'quicker and sicker' with higher levels of dependency and disability than before.
- Poor communication between community and hospital, before, during and after discharge.
- Lack of adequate assessment and planning.
- Lack of service support and provision and subsequent reliance on informal support from family and friends.
- Insufficient notice of discharge.

(Penhale, 2000, 2002; Phillips and Waterson, 2002; Davies and Connolly, 1995; Tierney et al., 1994; Fisher et al., 2006)

The division stems not only from professional orientation but also from the different knowledge base of the two sectors. The biomedical model in health care draws on what is perceived to be hard science and endows professionals with unquestionable authority, whereas social care is rooted in soft science and the sometimes disputed therapeutic tradition.

Medical practice is characterized by doing things to the body, often of an invasive nature, whereas social care is more nebulous – counselling or other interpersonal work or more mundane day-to-day tasks. People often believe that this kind of work can be done without training or specialist knowledge. Social care is often provided in situations that are not life-threatening, but it is important for survival, a pattern and quality of life. However there is a widespread notion that medicine and health care are vital but social care is optional. Differences in the use of technology also exist; technology can be seen as intrusive in people's lives, for example through surveillance and through medical intervention.

Different patterns of confidentiality and accountability between professions are also key areas of rivalry (Lymbery, 2005). Nurses will have different administrative tasks from social workers and will also be located in a hospital: this is where the ground-breaking advances are, not the community.

The different philosophies of care underpinning these two orientations – the medical and social models – have consistently posed dilemmas in our understanding and differentiation of care. The dominance of the medical profession in the arena of care has led to the inappropriate medicalization of social problems tying people into a dependency relationship. On a practical level it has also made working together fraught with difficulty. It has ramifications for the concept of care with the idea of cure and the medical model determining intervention and ways of understanding the need for care. Debates about the divide such as the above have been articulated by the disability movement and groups (including learning disability, physical disability, mental health, childbirth and terminal illness associations), all arguing to re-establish the significance of ordinary social life in both settings.

Glendinning and Means (2004) chart the history of the lack of integration between health and social care in an article questioning the current role of care trusts in providing the answer to long-term care integration. Despite recent attempts to introduce a National Service Framework (NSF) for Older People requiring collaboration, the legacy of the past fifty years has led to increased fragmentation. This, they argue, derives not only from the origins of the welfare state but also from the underfunding of preventative services for older people (located in local authorities) and a fixation with reducing waiting lists that prioritizes and concentrates attention on the NHS. This despite older people's preferences for a broader social model of care and for social services to promote their independence (Twigg, 2001).

Single or unified assessment was introduced as one way of bridging the divide yet there have been concerns about a uni-directional and bureaucratic assessment tool (Swift, 2002; Evans and Tallis, 2001). Similarly concerns surface around the NSF for older people in that intermediate care may develop into a cheap and substandard diversion from hospital access, with the risk that some of the standards would merely be 'cosmetic' (SCIE, 2005). Other evidence, however, demonstrates that there is value in an integrated approach (Johri, Beland and Bergman, 2003; Wanless, 2006).

Case study

It is in the area of ethics that working in partnership can come to the fore in dilemmas and decision making for social and health care professionals. Lucy and Jim have five children; Lucy is a heavy drinker and suffers from a psychotic illness which frequently results in hospital admissions under the Mental Health Act 1983. In a recent home visit by her community psychiatric nurse (CPN) following a return from hospital Lucy tells her that she no longer wishes to take her medication. A hospital nurse has seen her threatening her children and a social worker has become re-involved with the family because Jim has been recently absent from the family home following a local crime. Nursery services are restricted in the area and the social worker is faced with making a decision about priority of need with other families similarly in need. The hospital nurse is also wondering if she should report the threatening behaviour, breaking the trust that Lucy has developed with her over a number of years and the CPN has to make a decision in relation to monitoring and controlling Lucy's medication. Whose frame of reference should take priority in this case study? How should agencies work together in relation to this case study?

Care as paid employment

Professional debates around boundaries also operate in relation to carework.

Paid care extends to care workers working in care homes and day care centres and domiciliary workers caring in the community, thus providing a diverse context. In some sites workers will be working with others undertaking the same roles and with proximity to their manager; in other contexts workers can be isolated, rarely see colleagues and have sporadic contact with managers. As chapter 5 illustrated, care in the formal economy is mainly provided by women, a high proportion of whom are over the age of 50, working part-time in the private sector for low wages (Cameron and Moss, 2001). Recruitment and retention in relation to adult services is a key issue (Garthwaite Report, 2005), as it has been at different times in the nineteenth and twentieth centuries. Minority ethnic workers and migrants are increasingly being employed in the sector reinforcing existing low wages and low status and additionally introducing issues of culture, language and racism.

Home care is at the end of the continuum with 'family' or informal care where the worker operates within the space of the service user's home. The boundaries of private and public, professional and informal are blurred through the care being sited in a private sphere. The home in this context is no longer the private abode, where people have security and independence, but may be an arena for care to be reconceptualized and professionalized.

Qualitative data from Canada (Martin-Matthews and Mahmood, forthcoming) shows that boundary negotiation and management between workers and care recipients in this context is fraught with difficulty. They draw on the work of Nippert-Eng (1996) and Felstead and Jewson (2000) to understand these boundary issues of segregation and integration between home and work. From the home workers' point of view boundary conflict was associated with the invisibility of the work along with lack of status, role ambiguity and variability of the work and the switching of work between the realms of home and work – with home care workers developing a friendship role and working outside agency hours to meet the needs of a care recipient when required. Such affective ties lie at the heart of the issue. The relationship between public and private is compromised through the reciprocal emotional support between recipients and workers. It is this element of 'emotional labour' (Hochschild, 1983) which jars with agency guidelines and procedures. It is the negotiation of the emotional boundary which occurs in the 'intermediate domain' between home/private and work/public (Ward-Griffin, forthcoming; Martin-Matthews and Mahmood, forthcoming) and it is 'mediated by the structures of social, spatial temporal environment of the private residential setting and the organizational environment of the home care agency as well as the public health care system' (Martin-Matthews and Mahmood, forthcoming).

The relationship between the worker and care recipient is clearly important and provides job satisfaction for the worker (Mears and Watson, forthcoming). Care at home and care at work are seen as similar by some care workers, strengthening some care workers' sense of identity and giving them motivation to enter or continue in the caring business (Mooney and Statham, 2002).

> The overlaps moved towards a merger of work, family and self, so that all spheres were seen as united on the level of commitment and loyalty, but also on the level of content and what the job consisted of, its tasks, values and directions. This commitment and knowledge base can arguably strengthen workers' sense of identity as a careworker: caring is an ethic or a 'habit of mind'. (Cameron, undated, p. 15)

Although this would not be denied by the employing agency, being able to place boundaries that limit the extent of the involvement is a mark of professionalism. Yet emotional labour is at the heart of the work – being able to build trust and develop an empathic, warm and genuine relationship is vital to the delivery of any form of care. Drawing boundaries around this complex and diverse arena constrains care. This is however what bodies such as the General Social Care Council attempt to do in setting out their standards of practice. The process of delivering care can be as important to the individual as the specific outcome inasmuch as the caring relationship can be of greater value to the individual than the meeting of identified need. The extent to which the family can be the root or reference point of carework is increasingly challenged by the need for formal qualifications, police checks and the demonstration of competence.

As care has developed into a larger and more profession-alized activity, the role of the supervisor and management has increased and target-oriented practice has developed along with budgeting and increasing bureaucracy in meeting standards. Unlike the medical analogy where the consultant oversees the most complex cases, in social care it is the reverse; it is the care workers who work with the most complex individuals and situations, yet the power to make decisions remains within the management structure. A second or third tier manager may be so removed from the arena of the care worker and so detached from the individual service user that their decisions may appear more focused on the needs of the organization than on the need for care for the individual. The tensions between the managerial and care worker position can lead to stress for care workers with spill-over effects of their formal role on their informal caring relationships. This finding has been widely documented and debated in terms of juggling or balancing care (Phillips et al., 2002). Consequently there have been issues of recruit-ment and retention of the workforce in both social care and social work; it is the latter which is discussed below.

Recruitment and retention

The resource constraint environments of social services departments over the last twenty years have taken their toll on recruitment and retention, with the uncertainty of social work, stress and increasing responsibility leading to increased absenteeism (Moss and Cameron, 2001). Bureaucratization of care has led to stress and dissatisfaction. A Welsh report provides evidence that social workers feel undervalued, dis-satisfied with pay (particularly in relation to other profes-sions), supervision and office accommodation and have no clear career progression (Garthwaite Report, 2005). One of the ways forward will be to create a clear role for social work within the framework of social care, one that does not relinquish direct contact from service users and can lead to a mentoring or coaching rather than managerial progression (Garthwaite, 2005).

The erosion of what many see as the 'bread and butter' of social work, that is, the relationship between service user and the worker, has thrown into sharp contrast the distinctive role of the social worker. It can be argued that the professionalization of care remains in this domain with the roles and functions of social work located within defined responsibilities. Social workers act under certain legislation and are catalysts for the enactment of community care, children and family legislation and mental health legislation. The care management process also creates distinctive functions for social work in 'a way that promotes independence of service users and carers' and protection of socially excluded, isolated and vulnerable people in society (Garthwaite, 2005, p. 56).

Staff retention and turnover is a key issue with heavy workload, stress, low pay, lack of appreciation, increasing bureaucracy and poor supervision cited as reasons for leaving in the Welsh study (Garthwaite, 2005). Staff shortages have been increasingly filled by agency staff. This has serious consequences for the professionalization of care. If the profession places a premium on its relationship and continuity of care with service users then a 'revolving door syndrome' of staff leaving and temporary workers filling vacancies clearly raises problems. If care as a concept is to raise its status and if legislation is to be followed, for example in the Children Act 1989, then such difficulties have to be addressed. Care from a workforce which is dissatisfied, low paid, lacks support and has no long-term commitment to the job cannot be a recipe for enhancing either formal or informal care in society. The other side of the coin to this is the commitment that such social care staff have to their clients with many providing 'extra care' beyond that contracted.

Increasingly the debate is centring on the employment of migrant workers from recent accession states of the

European Union, along with the use of illegal immigrants in the care workforce. On the one hand such workers fill the gap in the provision of care, but on the other hand language, safety and abuse are surfacing along with issues of rushed care, loss of continuity and a higher incidence of injuries (Stone and Wiener, 2001; Callahan, 2001; Hussein and Manthorpe, 2005). Active recruiting from abroad has also resulted in a loss of skilled workers from poor countries. Fifty per cent of Zimbabwe's social workers are in the UK (Firth, 2006) and in some local authorities 40 per cent of front line staff are from outside the UK. Care staff originating from abroad are also subject to exploitation through low pay and dangerous working conditions (Huxley, Evans and Munroe, 2006). This is not an issue unique to the UK. Countries such as Japan, Germany, Italy, Denmark and the USA face identical challenges.

With the shortage of workers in the care arena other resources are sought. Grandparents are not only fulfilling roles in looking after grandchildren but are employed in paid work (Mooney and Statham, 2002); direct payments to carers are changing the nature of who does what for whom, with the potential for 'dirty tasks' such as bathing and toileting shifting into the paid care arena. Relationships service users have with their paid carers will however be different from the relationships they had with workers employed by traditional care agencies. Consumer choice, empowerment, independence and citizenship increasingly come into play in the concept of care.

At the beginning of this chapter the question was posed whether the ethic of care could marry with a managerialist agenda adopted by health and social care agencies. Scanning the literature on care management and practice on health and social care boundaries leads us to a pessimistic conclusion. However, within each professional grouping there is an increasing emphasis on empowerment and participatory approaches, looking to community development solutions (through Sure Start and the National Service Frameworks). Such approaches can give us hope that the professions will move towards embracing an ethic of care. It is to these issues that the chapter now turns.

Empowerment and participatory approaches

Empowerment and care can sit uncomfortably as empowerment implies that people have control and choice over their
lives (Morris, 1997). Such approaches are based on a citizenship and human rights culture where equality and diversity
are valued. An inclusive agenda is part of this approach.
Empowerment and participation, however, mean different
things to different people and sectors. Keeping older people
'independent' has been translated into a message of keeping
them fit and active whereas it should mean giving people
more choice and control over their lives. Empowered choice
also requires informed user involvement. Although older
people's expectations are changing, services to enable choices
to be made lag way behind (Audit Commission, 2004).

Some initiatives are in place to promote participatory
approaches to care in both adult and children's services. This
can be seen at one level through family centres and at a
policy level through the Children Act, 1989 (Aldgate and
Statham, 2001).

Evidence from research suggests that participation by
children and families in decisions about their lives and in
their assessments is variable. The exception to this is for
disabled children (Morris, 1997a; Mitchell and Sloper,
2002). However, research into adult social care reports that
users are satisfied with services: 'Person-centred and needs-
led assessments have led to care being tailor made for the
individual' (CI, 2003).

There has been a critique of the person-centred approach
from a number of sources. As argued in chapter 5 the emphasis on independence, citizenship and autonomy as well as
emancipatory practice does not fit with certain stages of the
lifecycle, for example with the end of life when people are
dependent. Lloyd (2004) argues that not enough attention
is paid to death in old age, with only a narrow range of
services available to allow people to die at home. It is also
a time of great inequality, where those who have resources have access to palliative care, and a time when it is
difficult for a person to assert their rights. She argues that

'the way concepts such as justice and autonomy are conceptualised leads to inequalities, lack of resources or political will' (p. 245).

The feminist ethic of care as a way forward is advocated by Lloyd (see chapter 5) but she stresses that the ethics of care approach does necessitate human agency and an understanding of the person's own perception of their situation. This requires a more in-depth assessment than a one-off visit can provide. The centrality of the interrelationship in an ethic of care is crucial in discussing autonomy and person-centred care.

Warnes (2006) criticizes the distortion of person-centred approaches on the grounds that it emphasizes user-oriented services with people designing their care rather than thinking of it in a holistic way that would incorporate psychosocial as well as environmental aspects.

The ecology of care

Human ecology is a framework that focuses on the contexts in which people live their lives. Its main premise is that people do not exist in isolation but in interaction with the physical and social contexts in which they live (Bubolz and Sontag, 1993). Interactions among people and their contexts are dynamic. Human ecology is 'concerned with the processes and conditions that govern the lifelong course of human development in the actual environments in which human beings live' (Bronfenbrenner, 1979, p. 1643).

Integration and partnership approaches are current issues in both policy (Sure Start approaches) and practice. Whereas adult services have 'hang ups' on the integration of health and social care, virtually to the neglect of the wider social context of social care, children's services have taken on a more ecological and holistic approach (for example through youth services, Sure Start), which has led to a non-stigmatizing provision of care. As demonstrated above, shared values and cultures are important for such a whole-systems approach. Taking values of empowerment and participation of service users and carers into a different paradigm is necessary in care if an integrated approach is to succeed. In children's services, as argued earlier, this has happened, taking the stigmatizing care label away by placing care within the mainstream of education and approaches to work. A legal responsibility on agencies such as education, housing and health as well as social services and independent agencies to work together to promote the welfare of children in the Children Act 1989 has spearheaded integration. It can be argued then that social care, mainly the remit of adult care, should focus more on the social than the welfare elements creating a more integrated spectrum of mainstream services in which people give and receive care as a normal part of everyday life (through transport, housing and shopping, etc.). Moving 'care' from a patronizing and protectionist approach of 'keeping safe' and 'looking after' to a more person-centred and self-determining approach has recently surfaced in policy and increasingly in practice. As Waine et al. (2005) argue, we need a value continuum which embraces notions of prevention as well as protection. Independence, dignity and respect are 'buzz' words and messages from all circles. Choice has been the leader. 'Not only are concepts changing but our language is moving from care to assistance; dependence to interdependence; from prevention to promotion; paternalism to partners; from experts to enablers and facilitators and "life allies"; from segregated services to accessing universal opportunities' (Jones, 2006).

Returning to the geography of care, we see history repeating itself with a mission to focus such integrated approaches at the local neighbourhood level. The Barclay Report (1982) with its emphasis on 'patch' or locality-based working advocated this notion over twenty years ago. The ecological approach also emphasizes the importance of social networks and social relationships. Local Strategic Partnerships, for example, have been established bringing together agencies from across the public, voluntary and independent sectors to deal with issues such as deprivation and social exclusion. Viewing older people, for example, as contributing citizens with valuable roles in their community and neighbourhood is part of the Sure Start for Later Life (2006) approaches of policy and practice.

The Barclay Report focused on the future of social work services. In the intervening years the demise of social work in this arena of care has accelerated. The ecological approach to care, however, can enable social work to regain a voice. Ray Jones in his remarks on Sure Start for Later Life (2006) illustrates that social work is important and central to this development through its 'commitment to social justice and human rights; its ability to place people in context; emphasis on valuing and not rejecting; recognition and development of people's strengths and skills rather than their weaknesses; its problem solving in partnership approach; ability to provide structure among chaos, ability to harness resources; being an ally in promoting independence and choice and protecting when necessary.'

The debate is now moving to how we achieve a better vision for social care based on the above. There are a number of fundamental shifts which need to take place in the professional arenas of care. To develop an ecological approach requires firstly, a greater strategic focus and corporate responsibility. Into the debate need to come land use planning, transportation systems, housing and community need profiling to enable mainstream services to be developed for all citizens. The regeneration of deprived areas provides an opportunity to envision a social care for the future and factor in systems for all citizens. Additionally there needs to be a better understanding of local communities and engagement with political structures within communities. Secondly, a greater engagement with work communities is required. Work is of central importance to most people's lives yet this is seen as marginal in relation to care. Thirdly, emphasis needs to shift to social care promotion in the same way as health promotion agendas have been favoured in recent years.

In practice this poses difficulties for social workers and health workers who are constrained by resources of time and money. Preventative services and promotion of well-being is an aspiration, yet the priority is on those most 'at risk' and this prevents efforts being concentrated on community development. This however could be the remit of social care workers who are within the community; greater access to the community as a whole could be one way of providing an ecological approach to care which also raises the status of carework. Tying this into the social inclusion agenda within communities may also pave a way forward for social care. The professionalization of care however can move in a number of directions: one is to a highly bureaucratized, competency-led concept with boundaries and structures. This would mean the care worker is a 'technician' working to prescribed procedures, continuing to have medium to low pay and low status, with an increasing reliance on the private market and the individual citizen to provide care. This is reinforced by assuming that migrant workers will fill shortages in the care economy. Such a move undermines the importance of relationship work and increases the vulnerability not only of service users but of workers, who may suffer racist abuse.

Dissolving the boundaries of care at an organizational, professional, locational (home-work) level and between the emotional and physical divide can go some way towards realizing the potential for developing a social ecological model of care based on an ethics of care approach.

9

The Risks of Care: Abuse and Neglect

Chapters throughout the book demonstrate that the concept of care is complex. To deal with such complexity we often resort to categorization, sometimes of a binary nature: care seeking versus caregiving; caring versus abusing or neglecting. Such binaries are socially constructed but are useful, helping us to comprehend the concept of care. Madness is a classic example, where the condition was treated right up to the eighteenth century with brutality and strictness because of the belief that it was self-induced (Jones, 1996). Care in this sense was seen as a 'moral treatment' (Butler and Drakeford, 2003). Today such treatment would be viewed as inhumane and would not be permitted.

This chapter looks at abuse and neglect in the care system but first explores the concept of risk, which is closely associated and which itself has been socially constructed. A number of the debates have been located within a social work framework. The need to protect society as well as allow individuals freedom and personal autonomy entail major compromises which have led to increased managerialism. Consequently the debates addressing care and risk within the professional arena have focused on risk assessment and risk management, with some of the main issues surfacing around how risk is defined and measured.

The concept of care has been reconstructed, boundaried and redefined through the concepts of risk, abuse and neglect.

Child care has moved to child protection; care of older people to the protection of vulnerable adults. This chapter looks at the debates surrounding these areas.

Defining risk

There are various forms of risk: risk posed to others or risk to oneself. Kemshall (2002) defines two categories of risk and a third which combines elements of both:

1. Risks which people pose to others: for example, paedophiles being released from prison; mentally disordered offenders and those with personality disorders. (An example here is Christopher Clunis, who murdered Jonathan Zito in 1992; the resulting Inquiry highlighted the whole system failure of mental health services (Ritchie, 1994).) The liberty of the individual can be limited to protect others.
2. Risks to which people are exposed, referring to those who are vulnerable to risk. Vulnerability is central to decisions in community care and work with older people. Risk is balanced against quality of life, rights and autonomy.
3. Risk including both elements: for example, people with severe mental health problems can be a risk to themselves and others and assessment is difficult as it must take account of both vulnerability and risk.

In all three definitions the risk of harm is assessed by considering the seriousness of action and the likely frequency of such action.

One of the reasons why the concept of risk is difficult to define is that risk is not a scientific, homogenous concept. One person's risk will be another's preference. Driving fast cars, for example, can result in death but can be exhilarating and give immediate gratification. Risks are therefore differently defined and are culturally based. Risk taken over a lifecourse may be reframed as 'resilience' if the risk has paid off in the face of adversity. It can be argued that the discussion around what constitutes risk has hampered the development of ways of responding to abuse and neglect.

Risk is understood as uncertainty about a future behaviour or event. It can be seen as a 'good risk' – taking a chance, such as buying a lottery ticket – or seen as unwelcome and harmful, for example probability of death as a result of a behaviour. Life is inherently risky; risks are associated with every behaviour and the risks of not acting may be as significant as the risks of acting.

Alaszewski and Manthorpe (1991) define risk incorporating both good and bad aspects as 'the possibility that a given course of action will not achieve its desired outcome but instead some undesired and undesirable situation will develop' (p. 277).

Increasingly in the professional and care literature risk is viewed in a negative light and equated with danger, great loss and pain (Parton, 1996). The media has a role in this definition of risk as good risks are rarely given publicity. Good news is no news. The media plays a substantial role in exposing risk as a major public concern which has repeatedly been demonstrated in relation to allowing the rehabilitation of paedophiles in the community. A further example which raised debates on the influence of the media arose in relation to 'pindown' (Staffordshire County Council, 1991) when a Granada television documentary escalated the issue of repeated abuse in children's homes from one of local importance to national scandal.

Whereas it may be easy in retrospect to look back at abuses of care and pinpoint the surrounding and impending circumstances, defining risks surrounding relationships and contexts of care can be difficult. Although the task of care standards agencies, for example in residential care, to evaluate 'good' and 'bad' care centre around outcomes in relation to quality of life, the voices of residents can take second place to more managerial and safety concerns. The risks of emotional abuse and neglect are difficult to identify during inspection visits to care homes, for example, particularly for those with cognitive impairment. Evaluating the quality of relationships, particularly in group settings, is fraught with difficulty. What makes 'poor' care and what constitutes risk, neglect and abuse are all parts of the same continuum.

Care and risk

The subject of risk and probability has been given considerable attention within fields as diverse as mathematics, insurance, health and criminal justice; however, there has been little theorizing on risk and care. Yet care involves taking risks. Risk is a part of everyday life from the macro, societal level through to the micro, individual level. Beck (1992) refers to societies as 'risk societies' and Giddens (1990) stresses that risk permeates individual identity and social relations. Beck argues that in the 'risk society' the norm is for safety and protection. As a result risk becomes a 'moral statement' of society (Beck, 1992, p. 176). He also argues that such risk is continually changing as we become reflexive in a postmodern world.

We all take risks and often underestimate the risks we take (Hood et al., 1992) but those under the care of or dependent upon others can be particularly vulnerable. It is often down to the state agency, professional and caregiver to balance those risks. Vulnerability is associated with people with cognitive or intellectual impairment or with age where there is a lack of knowledge or understanding. In general people are assumed to be personally responsible for the risks they take although in many circumstances an individual's decisions are either uninformed or ill informed in regard to the degree of hazard or risk they are subjecting themselves to. In a caring situation however the person's freedom of choice in regard to risk may be altered. Risk is often underpinned by an assumption that there is a lack of individual agency or ability to form judgements. A carer may offer only a limited range of options (or even a choice of accepting or declining care) or may provide their own (or their agency's) analysis of risk. In extreme circumstances the carer may make the decision on behalf of the individual. Consequently 'others' more powerful and knowledgeable and who can assess the risk intervene in its definition. Although the state establishes the legal framework, the definition, assessment and management of such risk has been increasingly charged to professionals. In such cases the policing role of the carer can sit uncomfortably with the notion of individual rights.

Care can involve a dependency relationship and can therefore be linked with risk in a number of other ways. The motivations (for example, private care home owners having to make a profit versus the quality of care), behaviour (allowing a child home to abusive parents), acts of care (emotional, physical – handling of frail older people), power imbalances (between social workers and service users) and processes in sustaining care involve risks to all parties.

The type and extent of risk taking may vary depending on its location in the care system; for example in residential care the risk of violence between residents or towards staff by residents can be considerable. The debate has centred on where children of abusive parents are best cared for after being abused. Institutional or residential care poses potentially more risks in terms of care. This is due to the 24/7 living environment; power relationships; potentially risky situations; poor resources; confusion and lack of knowledge about what to do; low staff morale; failure by management to see a pattern of events and treating individual instances in isolation (see Butler and Drakeford, 2003). Life in any environment entails risks but environments such as residential establishments that are meant to maximize safety may compromise independence and limit the individual's life experience, exercising caution in favour of protection. Often abuse and neglect takes place oxymoronically in a location or relationship of care. The globalization and commercialization of care has also meant increased risk as people move between countries and unregulated sectors of care.

The concept of care has been redefined as risk aversion and protection. This has happened as a result of scandals in the care system highlighting neglect and abuse rather than good examples of care practice. Scandal has shaped policy responses and has led to changes in the way the state relates to its duty of care. Only failures of care gain the attention of senior management, the justice system and the media.

Walsh et al. (undated) track historical policy changes in relation to children and people with a learning disability to demonstrate the changing perceptions of risk. Children were initially viewed in terms of risk and dangerousness (and parents were criminalized for failing their children) but are now perceived in terms of vulnerability and hence a welfare or protectionist approach is pursued. For adults with a learning disability the opposite is true, with their potential risk to society taking precedence over concerns about their vulnerability; the subsequent policy emphasis was on control and criminalization as demonstrated through the 1908 Report of the Royal Commission on the Care and Control of the Feeble Minded (p. 24). Although policy has shifted somewhat, Walsh and colleagues argue that another conflicting policy objective has been introduced, that of minimal intervention in family life, which along with the empowerment of service users leads to professionals having to take greater risks than before. This has led to debates around the right level of state intervention and who has responsibility and liability for the outcomes.

The state's role in avoiding responsibility when risk assessments go wrong can be charted in the numerous child abuse scandals and subsequent inquiries. The inquiry itself becomes an actor in constructing the framing of the problem and the response to it. Its first task is to establish whether an alleged scandal did take place and reconstruct the circumstances that led up to it; yet such apparent objectivity, as Butler and Drakeford (2003) argue, is only part of the construction. 'The conclusion we reach here is not only that there is no simple "truth", as many Inquiries claim, but that "truth" is influenced by the institutional framework within which the seeking-after it is conducted' (p. 221).

Rights and risks

Alaszewski and colleagues (undated) argue that the move from institutional to community care has led to a focus on the client's right to take risks yet at the same time there has been increasing intervention in the private sphere of the family to protect children from physical, sexual and emotional abuse as well as increasing risk management of those in the community who may be seen to be 'dangerous' under the 1983 Mental Health Act. Risk is placed within an individualist rather than a collective institutional framework, but abuse, for example, may have been more visible in the 'clearly identifiable location' of the institution (Alaszewski et al. undated p12). The individualization of risk does not only apply to families; blame and responsibility is placed at the feet of individuals when something goes wrong.

Since the nineteenth century there has been an emphasis on the individual in society and the centrality of the individual in decision making; this consequently has formed the basis for judgements to be made in relation to individual capacity and competence to take risks. Risk has shifted down to the individual level of decision making, reflected in practice through user empowerment and a broader participatory approach, and in policy by placing the responsibility on individuals for arranging their care, for example through direct payments. In the case of children it is related to parental responsibility and whether parents have the ability to assess the interests of the child.

Acceptability of risk is a crucial element in balancing rights and risks. Habermas (1991) evaluated actions by the degree of success or failure to achieve goals; by general acceptability morally, politically, culturally and legally; by honesty and genuineness of the decision or action; or according to what is understood or agreed or disagreed upon between participants about all of these points (Manthorpe et al., undated). The threshold between acceptable and unacceptable risk is finely balanced and subject to change. This is also the case with rights. In both the pindown and Cleveland scandals the issue of children's rights clashed with the notion of risk. Rights were being withheld in both forms of abuse (through a restriction on children's liberty and education) and in the resulting inquiries the issue of children's rights was held centre stage in the redefining of care.

Risk is central to professional practice (Alaszewski, Harrison and Manthorpe, 1998) and risk management is complex. Risk and uncertainty are managed through systems for organizing professional practice and mechanisms for predicting future risk and its consequences. Despite its complexity there has been de-professionalization of care (see chapter 8) with decision making in difficult cases resting with low-grade staff. Many would argue (Webb, 2001; Phillips, Ray and Marshall, 2006) that the task of risk assessment has continually been broken down into measurable and controllable parts leaving little room for professional judgement and more reliance on a competency-based approach.

The current system may also put people at risk because of staff shortages and the assignment of social work functions to untrained and unqualified staff. As the Garthwaite Report (2005) highlights:

> The increased expectations on local authorities to demonstrate performance have added pressure on social workers in a climate of limited capacity. The net result is one of increased public expectations and an inability to keep pace with demands. When this is at its most acute, mistakes happen, sometimes with grave consequences. (p. 107)

The 'blame' culture has arisen as a result of the delicate balance between rights and risks. Often professionals are balancing risk against choice, rights and responsibilities, rehabilitation, autonomy and quality of life. Drewett (1999) suggests there has been a lack of a theoretical base exploring the 'source and status' of rights (p. 166), accompanied by a confusion between rights- and needs-based approaches. This becomes even more difficult when establishing legal rights to social care, where the definition of care, let alone the entitlement to rights, is far from clear. Who should define needs and rights also raises thorny issues for translating this issue into practice and how to balance rights with risks. In relation to older people there is a risk of overprotection and on occasions the family's inability to cope with risk (for example, if an older person has sometimes left the gas alight) has compromised the older person's ability to remain at home, necessitating an admission to residential care. In child care the decision to leave a child in the potentially abusive family environment is a challenging one. Punishment is the penalty for getting the balance wrong between protection and control and autonomy and empowerment. This is often punishment at the level of the personal social worker or health worker as in the case of the inquiry into the death of Jasmine Beckford (London Borough of Brent, 1985, para. 287) where the media hounded the social worker involved in the case.

The debate regarding to what extent the state should intervene has often fallen to the social worker. Agency staff are blamed if they fail to protect (such as in the case of Victoria Climbié) or if they overprotect children (Cleveland Report, 1988) and if they fail to protect society from individuals deemed to be dangerous. In child abuse inquiries such as Cleveland, where children had been taken into care on the basis of a diagnosis of sexual abuse by two paediatricians, communication was at fault in addition to a lack of mediation between all parties and the lack of recognition of the complexity of risk involved.

In relation to learning disability the principle of normalization stressed the importance of giving people with a learning disability as normal and empowered a life as possible, which included taking risks far greater than they were allowed to take within the institution, an argument which persuaded some of the inherent benefits of institutional life.

Hood et al. (1992) argue that social services organizations are blameist organizations, allocating blame to decision makers and emphasizing accountability and bureaucracy. Inquiries play a major part in enabling the system to be rectified (Hill, 1990). The media has also taken a judgemental role in such situations, promoting a negative and blameist approach when decision making goes wrong and undermining professional confidence. Walsh et al. (undated) argue that this has led to a reaction among professionals, making them more likely to take a protective approach rather than an empowering one. Uncertainty is a key element in social work and risk is at the heart of that uncertainty. The decline in certainty of the social work role has led to increasing audit (Parton, 1996) leading in turn to new forms of organizational defensiveness. Despite legislation and guidance, mechanisms cannot be completely successful in protecting all children. This has been demonstrated on numerous occasions through the public scandals of Maria Colwell, Jasmine Beckford and Victoria Climbié. Despite the public inquiries that followed, mistakes have occurred.

Measuring risk

In the late twentieth and early twenty-first century there has been an increasing emphasis on risk management and the quest for objective measures. Unlike engineering, the care arena is hard to quantify and does not lend itself to being categorized in the same way. It is not possible to reduce situations to equations. As Alaszewski et al. (undated) comment, two distinctive approaches to risk management are first through insurance and the probability of disaster, and second by placing the responsibility for risk in the hands of professionals. The move to greater professional and managerial accountability is fraught with difficulties involving cultural norms and the role of culture in the social construction of risk. 'Risk perception is inherently multidimensional and personalistic, with particular risk or hazard meaning different things to different people and different things in different contexts' (Royal Society, 1992).

Objective measures are used by epidemiologists yet risk here is different; different because in child care and child protection there is a low rate of prevalence (Dingwall, 1989). Prediction is either impossible or unreliable. It is often in hindsight that risk is fully appreciated (for example in the Christopher Clunis case). There are no rules for prediction of abuse (Parton and Parton, 1989). Professionals or those with 'expert knowledge' however may offer a view which until 2004 was accepted. The trust vested in such opinions now cannot be accepted so readily. Medical science provided a reliable foundation for our knowledge on child abuse until Sir Roy Meadows' assessment of baby battering was brought into question. Such 'expert' advice no longer has the same authority and findings are now open to question.

The distribution of risk or more socially just ways to empower all citizens is a key area for debate. Risk can be discriminatory in this sense. It can be gendered. In elder abuse those generally abused are women over the age of seventy. In the 1920s and 1930s control was exerted over women with a learning disability because of fears that their promiscuity would lead to increased feeblemindedness in the population. The principle of normalization (Wolfensberger,

1980) and a move to community care redressed this but relied more on the community to control socially inappropriate behaviour rather than institutions.

With the development of the mixed economy of welfare, risks are also evident in the supply side of the care business. Since the Thatcher era the vagaries of the market have produced a fragmented and potentially vulnerable market in care, with many care home owners going out of business and being replaced with multinational companies. The economics of the care business has been risky. 'Between 1998 and 2001, registered beds in nursing and mental nursing homes decreased by 9.5 per cent and places for older people and mentally infirm older people in residential homes decreased by 3.2 per cent' (Darton, 2004). This has led to many older people losing their homes.

In competing for contracts in a lean market risks are taken. Balancing risk on both sides of the care relationship leads to insecurity and possibly abuse and neglect as balancing the books takes precedence over quality issues. Risk aversion can mean control takes precedence over care. Control can be operated, for example, by a home owner who restricts all residents' mobility by such measures as locking doors so that those with dementia cannot wander outside, rather than looking at individual needs for safety and security.

Redefining care following neglect and abuse

Child care scandals often lead to changes in policy and practice. New guidelines for professionals and changes to legislation can result without an evidence base to support them. Change as a result of consensus and planned policy development rarely occurs. In looking at the development of policy around child care we can see that it is in reaction to such abuses that care is redefined and reconceptualized. The Maria Colwell case is a good example. Parton (1985) argues that it made us see abuse as a social problem for the first time with child protection overlaying child 'care' and a plethora of guidance following in the wake of the scandal.

The private nature of care and abuse had been propelled into the public domain. The relationship between the state and the family (as well as social work) in relation to care was brought into sharp focus. The media, as in the Maria Colwell case, can play a role in reconstructing the notion of care and abuse and of what is acceptable.

Abuse and neglect of vulnerable adults has a less well developed evidence and theory base than its parallel in child care. Yet that is not to say there have been any fewer scandals exposing poor care. It was not until 1993 that abuse was recognized and a consistent approach demanded (Penhale, 2006). The debates have centred on the definitions of abuse and how to raise it to public attention given ageist attitudes and ambivalence in relation to the care of vulnerable adults.

In relation to learning disabilities the Ely hospital scandal led to the debate on care or cure. As Jones and Fowles commented, 'Institutions do not cure deviant behaviour, they perpetuate it' (Jones and Fowles, 1984, p. 11). At Ely, and a later scandal at Whittingham hospital in 1972 (where a nurse was charged with murder), the level of resources available for care of patients was inadequate, as was the calibre of the staff, some of whom had provided evidence of their own brutality in other establishments (Butler and Drakeford, 2003). As Butler and Drakeford argue, scandal followed by inquiry after inquiry did little to bring about improvement in institutional care. Instead it propelled the case for care in the community and the political ideology of a mixed economy of care in the community. Successive governments have not wavered from the policy of community care, leaving institutional care to the mercies of the private sector. Despite regulation, inspection and the production of guidance, for example Home Life (Centre for Policy on Ageing, 1997), institutions, even if smaller and badged as 'family care', have still provided the venue for the worst abuses of care.

Most abuse however is carried out in the home at the hands of family carers (Fitzgerald, 2004). Society does not view abuse of older people in the same way as it does if the victim is younger, in terms of acceptance, toleration of abuse and in terms of their lack of legal rights, particularly if they have cognitive impairment. Fitzgerald (2006) argues that it is possible 'to neglect abuse to a point near death without committing a crime because there remains a reluctance to legally define the circumstances in which one adult can be assumed to have taken direct responsibility for the care and well being of another' (p. 93).

Justice or welfare?

The lack of recognition given to older people also affects the way in which they are treated within the system. One of the difficulties in current debates on care and abuse is the antithetical positions of welfare and justice. In a number of instances where abuse of older people has taken place it is often not seen or described as abuse by the popular media. Brogden and Nijhar (2006) argue that emotional abuse in care homes is at the opposite end of the spectrum from murder (such as the Harold Shipman case). The failure of the criminal justice system to recognize abuse and victimization of older people has resulted from a number of issues. Among these are the difficulties in the definition of an 'offence, the artificial opposition between welfare and justice paradigms; the public/private space dichotomy' (p. 39), along with the ignoring of older people in victimology and the view of older people as a homogeneous group.

Brogden and Nijhar (2006) argue that the concept of 'zemiology' provides a way of moving beyond the discourse of welfare versus justice. Zemiology is an attempt to consider and integrate all negative aspects and consequences of behaviour in society. Brogden and Nijhar seek a comprehensive holistic view of social harm that encourages us to look beyond the current criminal offences and civil wrongs that can at present be taken before the law courts. A full acceptance of the concept of zemiology results in an understanding that many social phenomena that are not actionable at law are nevertheless contrary to the common good. Social justice and the protection of social harmony and order are goals to strive for while fully recognizing the inequalities that individuals are subject to and incorporating protection for the vulnerable. Thus failure to care and abuses of care are recognized and given due importance within a paradigm of zemiology.

Older people who abuse or are offenders are increasingly coming into the spotlight for debate. Should older offenders be treated as victims or criminals? Should they be treated in the criminal justice system or the care system? The focus on age and health and social care needs has been a factor in such decisions. In past years when a crime was committed by older people in the community it was often, and still is, a matter for social services to regulate rather than criminal agencies. A care and welfare rather than a justice and punishment approach pervaded (Thomas and Wall, 1993; Taylor and Parrot, 1988). Similarly there have been discussions about issues of health care, death and dying as they affect older people in prison (promoted in the media by the health of Ronnie Biggs). The question of bringing war criminals/sex offenders to trial many years after the event has also raised issues of older people, risk, frailty and criminal justice. Policy responses however have been reactionary, triggering debates about whether to segregate or integrate such prisoners on the basis of age (*The Guardian*, 30 January 2001).

Fitzgerald (2006) argues that the protection of vulnerable adults and older people should be seen within a citizenship framework. Residential support in the form of regeneration, social inclusion and supporting people would be helpful in casting off the image of older people as victims in need of protection and 'reinforce the mutual obligations (between individual and society) inherent in social inclusion policies' (p. 95). Policies around Sure Start for Later Life (Office of the Deputy Prime Minister, 2006) and other preventative measures highlight the wider citizenship approach based on collective citizenship where individuals can be active members in society with others. Cultural change is also necessary, however, to reframe care and abuse.

What does this say about care? Tronto (1993) argues that in some respects the notion of protection can be included in a definition of care but it is difficult to balance protection and the rights of individuals to take risks.

Case study

Lillian is an 80-year-old single woman living in a bungalow on the edge of a large town. She lives as a recluse, who rarely leaves the house, her only company being her dog. Environmental health officers have been concerned over several years at the state of her living conditions and on several occasions they have been required to work with social workers and impose section 47 of the National Assistance Act 1948, resulting in a compulsory removal to residential care. Social workers have attempted to work with Lillian over several years to motivate her to look after herself. Several psychiatric assessments have labelled her with a personality disorder. The constant dilemma for all those involved in the maintenance of Lillian in the community revolves around the risk she and her neighbours face in relation to their health and environment and the rights she has to live in such squalor. Additionally the personal risk to workers also has to be factored into any assessment. Recasting people like Lillian as vulnerable and in need of protection shifts the focus of social work from working on empowerment to risk aversion. There is a pressure on social workers to 'do something'. The issues for social workers are in balancing the rights of Lillian to live as she wishes with the risks to her and her neighbours; she is also vulnerable to abuse as well as self-neglect and the extent to which a protective function can operate has to be assessed – should a more appropriate living environment be discussed with Lillian? For social care workers who provide sporadic care to Lillian when she allows, the issues are whether they are obliged to enter such an unhealthy environment and place themselves at risk, as well as how to provide care to her in the most acceptable way without the fear of abuse.

Increasing risk of abuse and neglect has led to care being redefined as protection and people being recast as vulnerable. Professionals have to strike a delicate balance when making decisions between autonomy and empowerment and the rights of the care recipient versus protection. It is this delicate balance which forms considerable debate within professional arenas of care.

10
Reconceptualizing Care

This book has attempted to review the concept of care from a number of different perspectives. Some reflect traditional ways of looking at care, for example from a policy or feminist perspective; others, such as the geography of care, represent new and emerging areas for analysis. The book has not been exhaustive on all concepts and has not tackled issues such as the economics of care, technologies to enhance care, or care in particular situations and contexts such as hospice and palliative care at the end of life. Developments in all these areas, however, challenge our current conception of care.

The complexity, diversity and multiplicity of care have been continual themes. Care can be seen as a universal concept but there are tensions in that the diversity and complexity of care (its context, definition, recipients) means that experiences of care are not universal. The ubiquitous nature of care can also render it meaningless. The question is how should we approach care? The book has not attempted an overarching definition but has led the reader to look at how it has been conceptualized by different groups, ideologies and ideas over time – from a concept of dependency to that of citizenship. It has been defined in functional terms, associated with the medical model, characterized by people's age and gender, and been related to the social model and viewed as a social construction.

The boundaries between paid and unpaid, professional and personal, formal and 'informal', private and public are blurred. Given this blurring and complexity, is caring a useful concept or is it too diverse to be useful? Should we be reformulating a concept of care (as demonstrated in chapter 5), placing the concept within a citizenship model, or is it a concept beyond redemption and locked into a welfare/dependency paradigm? A redefinition of care is required for it to be a valued concept. This is one of the main debates which this chapter addresses.

What can be concluded is that the concept of care is situated in a postmodern, poststructuralist world which can be defined by uncertainty, where social relations are in a state of flux along with the uncertainty about the welfare state and the availability of services for carers and for those in need of care. In chapter 4, for example, the future care of a number of members of Edgar's family is more uncertain than it would have been fifty years ago when single daughters and those living nearby would have been expected to care; those without such family would have been expected to enter residential care if their care needs required it. Today family relationships and roles are negotiated on very different bases, not necessarily on obligation.

The characteristics of postmodernism are apparent in the care arena. The dominant cultures and organizations providing care are being critiqued. Chapter 8 challenged the definition of professional care and identified the power relationships guiding the concept of care. Care is being defined by dominant professionals but often disguised under the banner of person-centred care, empowerment and independence to suit political and ideological ends. In some respects these dominant paradigms make it difficult to move the debate on to one addressing care as a right and part of a citizens' contract. To some extent the welfare tag has been removed from child care where the concept of care has been reframed within a work rather than a welfare paradigm and set in the context of educational services. As chapters 4 and 5 highlighted, a work ethic needs to be balanced with an ethic of care.

Care is increasingly big business: with an expansion of the global economy large multinational companies provide institutions that replace retirement and residential homes.

Unless debates of the above nature are openly voiced then business will dictate, telling the consumers what they want. Care is vulnerable to the vagaries of the market in an unprecedented way. This issue surrounds the debate about the right balance of care between public, private and family and state as well as the market place. One policy challenge will be to control the private market through means other than legislation.

These trends toward the commodification of care also reflect the increasing consumption of care in the private market place and the fragmentation that is taking place in the supply of care and the professions that provide it. Life is more reflexive and people are defining their own perceptions and assessments of need for care. Participation in social care by individuals and business is paralleled by the development of consumerist and democratic approaches to the concept. The introduction of direct payments and technological advances have, for example, enabled people like Alice in chapter 7 to find her own care providers and make choices based on her preferences; yet the complexity of the care market makes risk difficult to assess.

Risk and risk assessment is also taking prominence and is redefining the concept of care to one of protection of vulnerable adults and of children. An industry is also developing out of the increase in information and technologies to assist in assessing risk. Sabrina in chapter 5 would be able to return to work if appropriate technologies at work and home could enable her to remotely monitor her sister's actions at home giving both security and regular communication to both. Janice in chapter 2 could go onto the internet and decide on her care providers, based on what they might cost and their availability to meet her needs; yet there will be risks involved in this and the fragmentation of the independent sector makes it an area of complexity.

Given this postmodern framework in which care now operates, what are the emerging debates on care and what are the key components in a reconceptualization of care?

Chapter 10 reviews this question and looks at the new and emerging debates. These debates fall into the context of care in terms firstly of future expectations and trends and secondly of the value base underpinning the reconceptualization of care. Some would currently argue that there is a crisis in care and that care is a concept past its sell-by date. Others disagree and argue that care is becoming more recognized and acknowledged in policy, practice and research.

Is there a crisis in care? Future trends and expectations of care

The pessimists would argue that there is a crisis in care on the basis of the following:

1 *Demographics and the demand for care*   An ageing population, particularly among the older population (those over 85), could mean increasing possibilities of disability and illness. Such factors accompanied by declining fertility, migration and geographic distancing, and the breakdown of families will mean increasing demand for care. Such demand will also come from groups of older people who previously did not survive into old age, such as those with a learning disability. Many will be from ethnic minority groups and will have dementia.

2 *Supply of care – the weakening role of the family?*   Patterns of change within families such as increasing divorce, increasing generational age gaps between family members and a decline in fertility all have severe consequences for the supply of informal care. Family norms and expectations are also weakening. Taken together with the stress carers face in juggling work and care and in caring for individuals with particular health needs, for example mental health or physical disability, the supply of care will be threatened. In relation to ethnic minorities there may be particular pressures in the family.

   The notion of ambivalence in intergenerational relations is central to the care debate. Both at a structural level (through balancing work and family life) and at a micro level of conflicting emotions and behaviours ambivalence is being acted out within care situations. Ambivalent relationships are increasingly being discussed in relation to adult care. Individuals may be unsure of the roles they play within families and beyond in relation to caregiving and care seeking. The contract of care may be viewed differently within a civil 'marriage' of same-sex couples, for example. The concept of ambivalence is not new in the literature on child care. Howe (2005) explores the ambivalent attachment style of parenting that can lead to an abusive or neglectful environment in which to nurture a child.

3 *Feminist debates – will women continue to care?* One of the main influences on defining the boundary of care has been the feminist debates of the 1970s onwards. Caring is highly gendered. However pessimists would argue that attitudes among women are changing with increasing opportunities for work. Women in the formal care system reinforce the low status of informal care as formal care is seen as an extension of domestic labour both performed by women and seen as women's natural domain.

4 *Location and distance* Geographic distance is an issue in the provision of care and there will always be a cut off in terms of how far carers can travel to provide certain types of care. Massey (2005) argues that space doesn't matter particularly as globalization and technologies of the future render geography less important. Debates highlighted in chapter 7 take issue with this view and advocate that geography does matter particularly where care is concerned, with proximity to social relationships and services of increasing importance. The concept of proximity is still crucial to care. This will be an increasing difficulty for 'only children' without extended family support in caring for older parents.

5 *Policy solutions are not attractive* The concept of care in policy has not been developed and debated. Policy has been reactive rather than planned and sustained by resources. Institutional care is a classic example, having had a chequered history, without

sustained investment; consequently the quality of care in residential establishments for children and adults has been poor. Difficulties in regulation and inspection of care make this a pessimistic arena for care in the future. Barriers within organizations and cultural systems remain and are expressed as problems at certain transition points, for example when children leave the care system and become defined as adults; when people are discharged from hospital; or when an older person has to enter nursing or residential care.

6 *Recruitment and retention difficulties*   Staffing difficulties in the formal sector of care will lead to the lack of an alternative quality solution to the family as carers. Family care will need supporting by formal services if the family is to continue as a viable unit in which to provide and receive care.

There is uncertainty about the funding of care because of the vulnerability of the market. Encouraging men to take on roles as carers will have to be introduced in the formal care system to address the recruitment and retention problems yet there are problems of low status and low pay in the formal sector.

7 *The costs of care*   The costs of care can be significant for the lifetime of care recipients and carers. The main debate has centred on the long-term care of older people and the rationing of care rather than the social and employment costs and pensions penalty to carers. The rationing of care around age is a very sensitive issue.

8 *'Care' is too complex and multidimensional to be easily defined*   The different ingredients involved in care and different understandings of care (multidimensional nature; tasks; what skills and abilities it involves; relationships and feelings; interdependency; emotional labour and multiple perspectives on care) make this a difficult concept to work with. The difficulties extend to establishing the boundaries of care, medical-social and the location of personal care, all of which are tied into the debate about who pays for what aspects of care.

9 *The needs of ethnic carers aren't addressed* The incidence of disability and illness are higher among certain ethnic minorities: for example sickle cell disease is more common among sub-Saharan African populations and their descendants. Demand for care may be high yet families may be dislocated through distance and culture. The high incidence of black children in the 'looked after' care system continues. Dual detachment is also apparent for older people who no longer feel attached to their home of origin or to their home of destination. Problems can exist over late migration back to the homeland where they may face the triple jeopardy of being old, disabled and out of cultural context (Norman, 1985).

Diversity and difference mean more tailor-made approaches rather than standardized provision, however children with disabilities and older people with mental health problems still face discrimination in these areas.

10 *There are risks of care* The risk to self and to others exists in all arenas of care – residential, home care and in the community. Care staff are also at risk, which is linked to the low status of their work. Yet risk has to be balanced with rights and responsibilities. It can be argued that the over-concentration on risk aversion among professionals in the health and social care fields stifles 'good' care promoting independence and empowerment.

Conversely there are optimists who argue that there is not a crisis in care. They see the pessimistic view as a social construction, fuelled by various interest groups. They identify the following as positive factors:

1 *Demographics* Older people are healthier and leading active healthy lives – positive ageing could mean less disability and dependency in the future. The need for care may lessen with medical advances even into late old age. The number of children in the care system is declining as the number of children in the population declines.

2 *Family care continues to be important in people's lives across the lifecourse* There is little evidence of a decline in family support. Williams' research (2004) highlighted the commitment to care within families. Changing structural and societal conditions are moving the concept of family care to one of 'intergenerational care' as longevity extends family relationships across a number of generations. The 'sandwich generation' of carers with older parents and younger children is talked about in workplace literature. On a structural level families are changing and becoming a multiplicity of different forms and relationships. Additionally there has been a strengthening of other relationships particularly among friends in care networks. New family forms are also emerging which may develop strong care links, for example lesbian relationships (Manthorpe, 2003).

3 *Diversity in sources of care* There is increasing gender diversity in care provision. Men are taking on care roles in parallel with the diminution of their role as the breadwinner. Services are also becoming more aware of the needs of ethnic minorities, gay and lesbian carers. New alliances are forming – traditional norms are breaking down through the diverse needs of women in work and the structure and loosening of blood ties within families and stepfamilies.

Highlighting cultural diversity and illustrating different models of care from across the world can challenge our dominant notions. This may enable the debate to take account of the diversity of care within the UK. Definitions of care and how they are manifest within different societies allow for different theories of what care is and how we assess good quality care.

In terms of formal services intermediate care, re-ablement services and preventative approaches are being developed as alternatives, enabling people to remain in the community.

4 *Good quality care* Quality care can be offered through promoting security, privacy, and an active educational

environment for children. The concept of care has become more positive with the stress on independence, empowerment and choice and less on care and need as a problem. Much of the book looked at the relationship between individuals, families and the state and where all these fit into the care jigsaw. The questions remain: to what extent should the state intervene when care is of poor quality and to what extent does the state regulate risk? Optimists would argue that increasing regulation will weed out poor examples of care.

5 *New technology will reduce physical geographical barriers* Caring can be performed at a distance through remote technologies. New innovations in environmental design and housing, for example smart housing, will allow remote monitoring and individual tailored response modes of providing care. 'Intimacy at a distance' (Rosenmayr and Köckeis, 1963) can be increased through the mobile phone and other technologies. People may also choose to migrate to be near sources of care – to children and services. First generation telecare systems such as social alarms have been found to be successful (Doughty, Cameron and Garner, 1996). The next generation based on a network of sensors in the home or on the body to monitor activities may provide carers and users with greater opportunities to provide personal care at a distance.

All these dimensions of care are bound together: for example, the care workforce shortage depends on the supply of carers from other countries, people's opportunity to care, family structures and their location. The future for the development of care will have components of each of these arguments. To understand the future demand for care services a number of other factors need to be considered. Emerging debates centre on technology and ethics; whether and how we ration care; how globalization will impact on care; and what values should guide our development of the concept.

New assistive technology and telecare

The concept of care is being challenged by technological advances that redefine care across the lifecourse. These include technologies from assisted reproduction to end of life decisions. New telecare systems which monitor body function, movement and daily activities such as cooking may be useful in indicating the general well-being of a person and enabling them to summon help quickly. It has been argued that the basis of a new 'caregiving system' could emerge (Guralnik and Haigh, 2002). To date there has been little discussion of the ethical issues of telecare – it has been embraced in the literature as a 'good thing' to assist in reducing costs as well as assisting carers and care recipients. Yet technologies are not neutral. As many of these new systems are not tested in relation to the mass market we know little of user acceptability and usage. There are dangers that the medical model will dominate the development of such technologies with an emphasis on the medicalization of care; the nature of articles in *Journal of Telemedicine and Telecare* highlight the possibility of this occurring. Increasingly the ethical aspects of these developments as well as issues of cost, rationing and eligibility will be central to any concept of care. Fisk (1997) believes that technology should not be perceived as a 'badge of dependency' but should be promoted in ways that affirm positive views of service users; control must be vested in the user, and the equipment and technology should offer the user additional facilities.

In looking back at the case studies in the book, technology at the workplace could assist Connie in chapter 4. Through remote monitoring she could keep in touch with Edgar while she works. Similarly technology at home can reduce the social isolation of people by connecting them to the outside world.

Mörtberg (2000) argues that 'The starting point of creating information society and IT strategies for future democratic practices must be in the civil society, in the everyday practices and situations'. Telework and IT have to be part of the increasing fabric of communications, opening up opportunities for all sectors of society and enabling individuals to gain information and make decisions about their care needs. Innovative projects in relation to the development of technology and citizenship in the Nordic states can be found via http://www.nuh.fi/nuh_uusi27052005/english/projekt. html.

Some (Tweed and Quigley, 1999) argue that technologies lead to increased dependency on them and can even mask dependency needs, possibly leading to social isolation. The issues for practice are therefore:

- a proper and appropriate assessment of an individual's need must be made and the technology must be appropriate to that need
- technology cannot replace face-to-face contact and this should be weighed up in the assessment of the use of technologies
- interactive technologies will become of increasing importance; social care workers will need to be informed and informative about the use of technologies in all contexts.

Rationing care

A crucial debate here is about rationing. On what basis can and should care be rationed? This is not a new debate within the health care field with the allocation of health care resources being linked to age. Callahan (1987) has argued that after reaching a 'natural life span', older patients should no longer receive life-extending therapies. Such ageist discrimination has been widely criticized as it does not consider quality and value of life or what criteria one can use to define a 'natural life span'. Increasingly evidence-based medicine – the idea that the doctor only prescribes therapies that have proved to be effective – is being used. The dangers apparent however are that cost-effectiveness is measured within these decisions and the decision itself is made by the manager rather than the doctor. In social care the primary argument is allocation on the basis of need yet fewer and fewer services are coming under this remit. Increasingly as services shift to the private sector, cost becomes a basis for rationing. For practice this raises dilemmas about need and eligibility for service provision.

Globalization

Globalization is a hallmark of the early twenty-first century with globalization of the economy seen as a solution to every country's financial and economic crisis (Chappell and Penning, 2005). A key component of globalization is the increasing disparity in relation to care along age, gender, class and racial lines. Global capitalism is being differentially experienced across the world and consequently having an impact on care systems (Navaroo, 2002). Yet some commentators, for example Lowenstein (2005), argue that the family remains an anchor for dealing with demographic, familial and social change. A key debate will be how inequalities arising from a global context can be tackled at a community and state level at the same time as giving families resources and freedom to act in care situations.

In relation to practice we have to factor in the existence of transnational families and that the wider context beyond the immediate locale can be a site for care. In such contexts the use of interactive technologies takes on added importance and can lead to greater flexibility and opportunities to care at a distance.

Social care values: the debates

We need a clear conceptual framework in which care can be publicly debated. This is long overdue. The debate needs to be clearly articulated around the values underpinning social care.

From needs to rights

In relation to children, Waine et al. (2005) in *Developing Social Care: values and principles* suggest debates around children and families have been characterized by explicit discussions about values and ideology centring on 'the child/family/state relationship; the need for children to be protected (prompted by repeated "scandals"); and concerns about the rights of children' (p. 4). The interests of the child are primary in decision making, paramount responsibility rests with the family, and partnership working between the state and the family is required under the Children Act 1989.

The shift in emphasis to *all* children (rather than those in need of protection, for example) in *Every Child Matters* (DfES, 2003) mirrors thinking in relation to the social inclusion and the human rights agendas. In children's legislation and practice the UN Convention on the Rights of the Child 1989 and the Human Rights Act 1998 have had a great influence. That children are valued in their own right and are able to make decisions about their future is embodied in *The Charter of Fundamental Rights of the European Union* (Euronet, 2000) and *Every Child Matters*. The primacy of the family as the best place for children to grow up is further echoed in Article 8 of the Human Rights Act 1998.

Whereas the human rights framework impacts on children's services, the same is not true for adult care where the social model has more relevance. However, the human rights framework is relevant to all users of adult social care, with its focus on inclusion and non-discrimination. A human rights framework can be one suited to a social model of care and can provide a universal approach to care across the lifecourse.

Whereas in the past care has been linked to need alone, increasingly the debates centre on the linkages of care and rights. The concept of need is also being reframed in a more positive light, moving from the view of need as a problem to one in which it is seen as socially constructed and about choice and control. Increasingly there is a broad consensus that what people want from social care is an emphasis on rights and a shift to user and carer influence and power. This has been mirrored in the modernizing agenda of the government 'putting people at the centre of public services'.

Social inclusion

Social inclusion is another building block for social care. Wistow (2005) notes that the debates on adult social care were framed in terms of social inclusion, empowerment and diversity, yet values such as citizenship and social inclusion emphasized the social obligations of citizens and the ethic of work rather than their rights and the ethic of care. 'There is considerable ambiguity both about their underlying definitions and about the extent to which they describe current practice or represent aspirations for the future' (p. 11).

As Phillipson and Scharf (2005) comment, 'community care should be refocused on social inclusion including the capacity of communities to support and sustain inter-dependent/independent living' (p. 65). The promotion of social inclusion is a form of low-level preventative service, emphasizing the shift from a focus on people with complex needs to the inclusion of promoting well-being. Increasingly this emphasis is being seen in the move to develop sustainable communities. The ecological approach described in chapter 8 is illustrated in policy and practice through Sure Start and Better Government for Older People initiatives in England and *Fullfilled Lives, Stronger Communities* in Wales.

Human rights, social inclusion and community capacity building are therefore identified as central elements in the future of social care. Values are shifting from individualistic notions to ones founded more on collectivism and citizenship.

A key practice issue is the extent to which we can develop sustainable care-friendly communities and environments that are suitable to all ages and needs, rather than age-based communities such as retirement communities.

Citizenship and an ethic of care

Lister (1997) argues that citizenship should be rooted in difference and along pluralist lines. She argues neither for equality with men in a gender-neutral approach nor for a gender-differentiated model but for a theoretical model that embraces both sides of the divide – the ethic of justice and the ethic of care. The debate is how to marry these two paradigms.

Throughout the book I have highlighted the blurring of boundaries between public and private, paid and unpaid, work and family life, between carer and care recipient on a practical as well as a theoretical level. A model of care based on citizenship principles needs to cut across the formal and informal, paid and unpaid divisions in the literature and absorb a number of contexts and care groupings. Additionally it needs to incorporate firstly a partnership approach based on empowerment and secondly the concept of the 'construction of difference' (Brechin, 1998, p. 182) which should not necessarily be viewed as negative, but can lead to good care if difference (in lifestyle, opportunity and agency) is supported and valued and is satisfying for both parties (ibid., p. 184).

This model in part would get us nearer to what was argued in chapter 3 highlighting the development of the citizenship approach and taking care beyond its boundaries in a welfarist and dependency relationship. This would free the family from being locked into a care relationship and allow and value caring across generations and involving others outside the family. However, as Sevenhuijsen (1998) argues in *Citizenship and the Ethics of Care*, citizenship should be revised from a rights-based status into a notion of citizenship based on agency and responsibility.

Dependency is part of life; we are all vulnerable and at some point in our lives will need care. Policy that stresses 'active ageing' and independence fails to recognize a lifecourse approach where vulnerability and dependency are episodically experienced. Caregiving is also part of everyone's life. We must not however fall into the trap that 'care is everywhere' (Sevenhuijsen, 2000) and render it a meaning-less concept.

For social care practitioners and nurses who work with people with care dependency needs these are important considerations; they often come across such needs in the context of vulnerability and dependency, yet this is only one point in time or snapshot of a person's life; the broader context of their lives needs considering.

As Daly and Lewis (2000), Tronto (1993), Williams (2001) and Sevenhuijsen (1998) all argue from slightly different viewpoints, care has to be central to the social fabric of society and a key reference point in policy. 'The feminist ethic of care offers a new conceptualisation of equity, justice and autonomy' (Lloyd, 2004, p. 247). Locating care within a citizenship framework provides us with a refreshing approach to reconceptualizing care.

A holistic and ecological approach across the lifecourse is imperative in policy. Care needs to be considered as integral to the development of agencies such as housing, education and learning, urban and rural planning, and health. Looking at care as it relates to these areas, and applying the four elements of Tronto and Fisher's definitions of care (attentiveness, responsibility, competence, responsiveness) would enable society to be more inclusive (Sevenhuijsen, 2000).

There are a number of central features however that are constant throughout these debates. Propositions that are central to the reconceptualization of care include:

1 Care is part of a relationship constituted through family and social relations and mediated through environment and culture. The spaces and places of caring and the cultural sensitivities of caring are of increasing importance.
2 There are multiple and complex forms of caring.
3 Care is a social construction. It is also marketed, packaged and sold.

This is a crucial time when moral boundaries are being redrawn. An 'ethics of care' needs to be publicly debated.

Closing reflections

This book has reviewed and tracked the main debates and approaches to care. It is a concept that is continually being re-evaluated and elaborated.

The debates and the ideas summarized in this book are important to those who formulate and influence policy and care practices. People act and react to care depending on how they perceive it – as a normal part of life or a dependency to be avoided. Images of care, in all forms of media and in how people experience care for themselves or their families and friends, will influence such perceptions.

Evidence from research still needs to be developed in the social care field, particularly in relation to outcomes for service users, carers and others, and particularly over the long term. Multi-method and multidisciplinary research is crucial in building a picture of good quality care. Defining and evaluating the concept of care will be increasingly crucial in this respect.

References

Acheson, D. (1998) *Independent Inquiry into Inequalities in Health*, London: HMSO.

Age Concern (1999) *Paying for Age in the 21st Century*, The Millennium Papers Debate of the Age, London: Age Concern.

Ahmad, W. (1996) Family obligations and social change among Asian communities, in W. Ahmad and K. Atkin (eds) *Race and Community Care*, Buckingham: Open University Press, 51–72.

Alaszewski, A., Harrison, L. and Manthorpe, J. (eds) (1998) *Risk, Health and Welfare*, Buckingham: Open University Press.

Alaszewski, A. and Manthorpe, J. (1991) Measuring and managing risk in social welfare, *British Journal of Social Work*, 21, 277–90.

Alaszewski, A., Walsh, M., Manthorpe, J. and Harrison, L. (undated) Health professionals and vulnerable individuals: managing risk in the city. Working papers on risk and social welfare, Institute of Health Studies, The University of Hull.

Aldgate, J. and Statham, J. (2001) *The Children Act: new messages from research*, London: HMSO.

Aldous, J. and Klein, D. (1991) Sentiment and services: models of intergenerational relationships in mid-life, *Journal of Marriage and the Family*, 53, 595–608.

Allan, G. and Crow, G. (2000) *Families, Households and Society*, Basingstoke: Palgrave.

Allen, I. and Perkins, S. (eds) (1995) *The Future of Family Care for Older People*, London: HMSO.

Andrews, G. and Phillips, D. (2000) Moral dilemmas and the management of private residential homes: the impact of care in the community reforms in the UK, *Ageing and Society*, 20, 599–622.

Antonucci, T. and Akiyama, H. (1987) Social networks in adult life: a preliminary examination of the convoy model, *Journal of Gerontology*, 4, 519–27.

Arber, S. and Ginn, J. (1991) *Gender and Later Life: a sociological analysis of resources and constraints*, London: Sage.

Arber, S. and Ginn, J. (1995) *Connecting Gender and Age*, Buckingham: Open University Press.

Atkin, K. and Rollings, J. (1992) Informal care in Asian and Afro-Caribbean communities, *British Journal of Social Work*, 22, 405–18.

Atkin, K. and Rollings, J. (1993) *Community Care in a Multi-racial Britain: a critical review of the literature*, London: HMSO.

Audit Commission (2004) *Older People: building a strategic approach, independence and well-being 2*, London: Audit Commission.

Augé, M. (1995) *Introduction to an Anthropology of Supermodernity*, London: Verso Books.

Azmi, S. (1997) Professionalism and social diversity, in R. Hugman, M. Peelo and K. Soothill (eds) *Concepts of Care Developments in Health and Social Welfare*, London: Arnold, 102–21.

Bach, M. and Rioux, M. (1996) Social well being: a framework for quality of life research, in R. Renwick, I. Brown and M. Nagler (eds) *Quality of Life in Health Promotion and Rehabilitation: conceptual approaches, issues and applications*, Thousand Oaks, CA: Sage.

Balbo, L. (1987) Crazy quilts: rethinking the welfare state debates from a woman's point of view, in A. Showstack Sassoon (ed.) *Women and the State*, London: Hutchinson, 45–71.

Baldock, C.V. (2000) Migrants and their parents: caregiving from a distance, *Journal of Family Issues*, 21, 205–24.

Baldock, J. and Ely, P. (1996) Social care for the elderly in Europe: the central problem of home care, in B. Munday and P. Ely (eds) *Social Care in Europe*, Hemel Hempstead: Prentice Hall/Harvester Wheatsheaf, 195–225.

Baldock, J. and Ungerson, C. (1994) *Becoming Consumers of Community Care: households and the mixed economy of welfare*, York: Joseph Rowntree Foundation.

Baldwin, S. (1995) Love and money: the financial consequences of caring for an older relative, in I. Allen and S. Perkins (eds) *The Future of Family Care for Older People*, London: HMSO.

Baldwin, S. and Twigg, J. (1991) Women and community care – reflections on a debate, in M. McClean and D. Groves (eds) *Women's Issues in Social Policy*, London: Routledge, 117–35.

Barclay Report (1982) *Social Workers: their role and tasks*, London: Bedford Square Press.

Barn, R. (2006) *Research and Practice Briefings: children and families – improving services to meet the needs of minority ethnic children and families*, DfES. http://www.rip.org.uk/publications/researchbriefings.asp.

Barnes, M. (1997) *Care, Communities and Citizens*, London: Longman.

Barth, F. (1969) (ed.) *Ethnic Groups and Boundaries: the social organisation of cultural difference*, London: Allen and Unwin.

Bauld, L., Chesterman, J., Davies, B., Judge, K. and Mangalore, R. (2000) *Caring for Older People: an assessment of community care in the 1990s*, Aldershot: Ashgate.

Bayley, M. (1973) *Mental Handicap and Community Care*, London: Routledge and Kegan Paul.

Beck, U. (1992) *Risk Society: towards a new modernity*, London: Sage.

Becker, S., Aldridge, J. and Dearden, C. (1998) *Young Carers and Their Families*, Oxford: Blackwell Science.

Begum, N. (2006) *Doing it for Themselves: participation and black and minority ethnic service users*, Social Care Institute of Excellence. Participation Report 14, London: SCIE and REU.

Bell, D. and Bowes, A. (2006) *Financial Care Models in Scotland and the UK*, York: Joseph Rowntree Foundation.

Bengtson, V. (2001) Beyond the nuclear family: the increasing importance of multigenerational bonds, *Journal of Marriage and the Family*, 63, 1–16.

Bengtson, V., Giarrusso, R., Mabry, B. and Silverstein, M. (2002) Solidarity, conflict and ambivalence: complementary or competing perspectives on intergenerational relationships? *Journal of Marriage and the Family*, 64, 568–76.

Bengtson, V. and Roberts, R. (1991) Intergenerational solidarity in ageing families: an example of formal theory construction, *Journal of Marriage and the Family*, 53, 856–70.

Beresford, P. (2004) Madness, distress, research and a social model, in C. Barnes and G. Mercer (eds) *Implementing the Social Model of Disability: theory and research*, Leeds: The Disability Press.

Beresford, P., Sloper, P., Baldwin, S. and Newman, T. (1996) *What Works in Services for Families with a Disabled Child?* Ilford: Barnardos.

Bernard, M. and Phillips, J. (2007) Working carers of older adults: what helps and hinders in juggling work and care? *Community Work and Family*, 10, 139–60.

Blakemore, K. (1997) From minorities to majorities: perspectives on culture, ethnicity and ageing in British gerontology, in A.

Jamieson, S. Harper and C. Victor (eds) *Critical Approaches to Ageing and Later Life*, Buckingham: Open University Press, 27–39.

Blakemore, K. (1999) International migration in later life: social care and policy implications, *Ageing and Society*, 19, 761–75.

Blakemore, K. and Boneham, M. (1994) *Age, Race and Ethnicity*, Buckingham: Open University Press.

Blaxter, M. (1976) *The Meaning of Disability*, London: Heinemann.

Boaz, R. and Hu, J. (1997) Determining the amount of help used by disabled elderly persons at home: the role of coping resources, *Journal of Gerontology: Social Sciences*, 52B, 6, S317–S324.

Bogdan, R. and Taylor, S.J. (1989) Relationships with severely disabled people: the social construction of humanness, *Social Problems*, 36 (2), 135–48.

Bornat, J., Dimmock, B., Jones, D. and Peace, S. (1999) Stepfamilies and older people: evaluating the implications of family change for an ageing population, *Ageing and Society*, 19, 239–61.

Bott, E. (1950) *Family and Social Networks*, London: Tavistock.

Bourdieu, P. (1990) *In Other Words: essays towards a reflexive sociology*, Cambridge: Polity.

Bowlby, J. (1980) *Attachment and Loss*, London: Pimlico.

Bowling, A., Farquhar, M. and Browne, P. (1991) Life satisfaction and association with social networks and support variables in three samples of elderly people, *International Journal of Geriatric Psychiatry*, 6, 549–6.

Braithwaite, V. (1990) *Bound to Care*, Sydney: Allen and Unwin.

Brannen, J. (2002) *Lives and Time: a sociological journey*, London: Institute of Education.

Brannen, J. and Heptinstall, E. (2003) Concepts of care and children's contribution to family life, in J. Brannen and P. Moss (eds) *Rethinking Children's Care*, Buckingham: Open University Press, 183–97.

Brannen, J. and Moss, P. (2003) Concepts, relationships and policies, in J. Brannen and P. Moss (eds) *Rethinking Children's Care*, Buckingham: Open University Press, 1–22.

Brechin, A. (1998) What makes for good care? in A. Brechin, J. Walmsley, J. Katz, and S. Peace (eds) *Care Matters: concepts, practice and research in health and social care*, London: Sage, 170–88.

Brody, E. (1981) Women in the middle and family help to older people, *The Gerontologist*, 21, 471–80.

Brody, E., Johnson, P., Fulcomer, M. and Lang, A. (1983) Women's changing roles and help to elderly parents: attitudes of three generations of women, *Journal of Gerontology*, 38, 597–607.

Brogden, M. and Nijhar, P. (2006) Crime, abuse and social harm: toward an integrated approach, in A. Wahidin and M. Cain (eds) *Ageing, Crime and Society*, Cullompton: Willan Publishers, 90–107.

Bromley, Y. (1989) The theory and ethnos and ethnic processes in Soviet social science, *Comparative Studies in Society and Social Science*, 31, 425–38.

Bronfenbrenner, U. (1979) *The Ecology of Human Development: experiments by nature and design*, Cambridge, MA: Harvard University Press.

Bubolz, M. and Sontag, M. (1993) Human ecology theory, in P. Boss and W. Doherty (eds) *Sourcebook of Family Theories and Methods: a contextual approach*, New York: Plenum Press, 419–50.

Burholt, V. and Wenger, G.C. (2003) *Families and Migration: older people from South Asia*. First Final Report, Bangor: Centre for Social Policy Research and Development, Institute of Medical and Social Care Research, University of Wales.

Bury, M. (2000) A comment on the ICIDH2, *Disability and Society*, 15, 1073–7.

Butler, I. (2000) Foster care, in M. Davies (ed.) *The Blackwell Encyclopaedia of Social Work*, Oxford: Blackwell, 138–40.

Butler, I. and Drakeford, M. (2003) *Social Policy, Social Welfare and Scandal: how British public policy is made*, Basingstoke: Palgrave Macmillan.

Butt, J. and Moriarty, J. (2004) Social support and ethnicity in old age, in A. Walker and C. Hennessey (eds) *Growing Older: quality of life in old age*, Buckingham: Open University Press, 167–87.

Bytheway, W. (1987) *Informal Care Systems: an exploratory study with the families of older steel workers in South Wales*, York: Joseph Rowntree Foundation.

Bytheway, W. and Johnson, J. (2005) Cataloguing old age, in G. Andrews and D. Phillips (eds) *Ageing and Place: perspectives, policy, practice*, London: Routledge, 176–87.

Bywaters, P., Ali, Z., Fazil, Q., Wallace, L. and Singh, G. (2003) Attitudes towards disability amongst Pakistani and Bangladeshi parents of disabled children in the UK: considerations for service providers and the disability movement, *Health and Social Care in the Community*, 11, 502–9.

Calasanti, T. (1993) Introduction: a socialist-feminist approach to aging, *Journal of Aging Studies*, 7, 117–31.

Calasanti, T. (2003) Masculinities and care work in old age, in S. Arber, K. Davidson and J. Ginn (eds) *Gender and Ageing: changing roles and relationships*, Buckingham: Open University Press, 15–31.

Callahan, D. (1987) *Setting Limits: medical goals in an ageing society*, New York: Simon and Schuster.

Callahan, J. (2001) Policy perspective on workforce issues and care of older people, *Generation*, 25, 12–16.

Cameron, C. (2003) An historical perspective on changing child care policy, in J. Brannen and P. Moss (eds) *Rethinking Children's Care*, Buckingham: Open University Press, 80–96.

Cameron, C. (undated) *Care workers' combining work and family: a case of merging identity*, unpublished paper, London: Thomas Coram Research Unit.

Cameron, C. and Moss, P. (2001) National Report, United Kingdom. WP3. Mapping of Care Services and the Care Workforce, *Care Work: current understandings and future directions in Europe*, London: Thomas Coram Research Unit.

Campbell, J. and Oliver, M. (1996) *Disability Politics: understanding our past, changing our future*, London: Routledge.

Campbell, L. (2000) Caring sons: exploring men's involvement in filial care, *Canadian Journal on Aging*, 19, 57–79.

Campbell, L. and Martin-Matthews, A. (2003) The gendered nature of men's filial care, *Journal of Gerontology: Social Sciences*, 58B, S350–S358.

Carers UK (2001) *It Could Be You: the chances of becoming a carer*, London: Carers UK.

Cartier, C. (2003) *The Chinese Diaspora: space, place, mobility and identity*, London: Routledge.

Centre for Policy on Ageing (1984) *Home Life: a code of practice for residential care*, London: CPA.

Centre for Policy on Ageing (1997) *A Better Home Life: a code of good practice for residential and nursing home care. Report of an advisory group convened by the Centre for Policy on Ageing and chaired by Kina, Lady Avebury*, London: CPA.

Challis, D. (1999) Assessment and care management: developments since the community care reforms, in M. Henwood and G. Wistow (eds) *With Respect to Old Age 69–86, Research Volume 3*, Cm 4192 11/3, London: HMSO.

Challis, D. and Davies, B. (1986) *Case Management in Community Care: an evaluated experiment in the home care of the elderly*, Aldershot: Gower.

Chappell, N. and Penning, M. (2005) Family caregivers: increasing demands in the context of 21st-century globalization? in M.

Johnson (ed.) *The Cambridge Handbook of Age and Ageing*, Cambridge: Cambridge University Press, 455–62.

Chau, R. and Yu, S. (2000) Chinese older people in Britain: double attachment to double detachment, in A. Warnes, L. Warren, and M. Nolan (eds) *Care Services for Later Life: transformations and critiques*, London: Jessica Kingsley.

Chodorow, N. (1978) *The Reproduction of Mothering: psychoanalysis and the sociology of gender*, Berkeley: University of California Press.

Chodorow, N. (1989) *Feminism and Psychoanalytical Theory*, Yale: Yale University Press.

CI (2003) 14: Improving older people's services – an overview of performance, DH SSI.

CIN (2001) http://www.dh.gov.uk/PublicationsAndStatistics/Statistics/StatisticalDevelopment/ChildrenInNeed/fs/en

Clark, H., Dyer, S. and Horwood, J. (1998) *That Bit of Help*, Bristol: Policy Press.

Cleveland Report (1988) *Report of the Inquiry into Child Abuse in Cleveland 1987*, presented to the Secretary of State for Social Services by Rt Hon. Lord Justice Butler-Sloss, Cm 412, London: HMSO.

Cockett, M. and Tripp, J. (1994) *The Exeter Family Study: family breakdown and its impact on children*, Exeter: Exeter University Press.

Connidis, I. (2001) *Family Ties and Aging*, Thousand Oaks, California: Sage.

Connidis, I.A. and McMullin, J. (2001) Negotiating family ties over three generations: the impact of divorce. Presentation to the IAG Symposium *Negotiating Intergenerational Relations Across the Lifecourse: Interpersonal, Theoretical and Policy Perspectives, Vancouver, July*.

Connidis, I.A. and McMullin, J. (2002) Sociological ambivalence and family ties: a critical perspective, *Journal of Marriage and the Family*, 64, 558–67.

Coontz, S. (2000) Historical perspectives on family diversity, in D. Derns, K. Allen and M. Fine (eds) *Handbook of Family Diversity*, New York: Oxford University Press, 15–31.

Corby, B. (2000) Looked after children, in M. Davies (ed.) *The Blackwell Encyclopaedia of Social Work*, Oxford: Blackwell, 199–200.

Culley, L. (2006) Transcending transculturalism? Race, ethnicity and health-care, *Nursing Inquiry*, 13, 144–53.

Daatland, S. and Herlofson, K. (2003) 'Lost solidarity' or 'changed solidarity': a comparative European view of normative family solidarity, *Ageing and Society*, 23, 537–60.

Dalley, G. (1988) *Ideologies of Caring: rethinking community and collectivism*, 2nd edition, London: Macmillan.

Daly, M. (ed.) (2001) *Care Work: the quest for security*, Geneva: International Labour Office.

Daly, M. and Lewis, J. (2000) The concept of social care and the analysis of contemporary welfare states, *British Journal of Sociology*, 51, 281–98.

Darton, R. (2004) What types of home are closing? The characteristics of homes which closed between 1996 and 2001, *Health and Social Care in the Community*, 12, 254–64.

Davies, M. and Connolly, J. (1995) The social worker's role in the hospital, *Health and Social Care in the Community*, 3, 301–9.

De Jong, G.F., Wilmoth, J.M., Angel, J.L. and Cornwell, G.T. (1995) Motives and the geographic mobility of very old Americans, *Journal of Gerontology: Social Sciences*, 50B, S395–S404.

Department of Health (1989) *Caring for People: community care in the next decade and beyond*, Cm 849, London: HMSO.

Department of Health (1998) *Modernising Social Services: promoting independence, improving protection, raising standards*, London: HMSO.

Department of Health (1999a) *Caring about Carers: a national strategy for carers*, London: Department of Health.

Department of Health (1999b) *National Service Framework for Mental Health*, London: HMSO.

Department of Health (2000) *The NHS Plan: a plan for investment, a plan for reform*, London: HMSO.

Department of Health (2001) *National Service Framework for Older People*, London: Department of Health.

Department of Health (2002) *Fair Access to Care Services: guidance on eligibility criteria for adult social care*, London: Department of Health.

Department of Health and Social Security (1978) *A Happier Old Age*, London: HMSO.

Department of Health and Social Security (1981) *Growing Older*, Cmnd 8173, London: HMSO.

DETR (2000) Index of Deprivation, London.

Department for Education and Skills (DfES) (2003) *Every Child Matters: Government proposals for childcare reform*, London: HMSO.

Dewit, D., Wister, A. and Burch, T. (1988) Physical distance and social contact between elders and their adult children, *Research on Aging*, 10, 56–80.

Dingwall, R. (1989) Some problems about predicting child abuse and neglect, in O. Stevenson (ed.) *Child Abuse: public policy and professional practice*, Hemel Hempstead: Harvester Wheatsheaf.

Doughty, K., Cameron, K. and Garner, P. (1996) Three generations of telecare of the elderly, *Journal of Telemedicine and Telecare*, 2, 71–80.

Drewett, A. (1999) Social rights and disability: the language of 'rights' in community care policies, *Disability and Society*, 14, 115–28.

Ehrenreich, B. and Hoschild, A. (2002) *Global Woman: nannies, maids and sex workers in the new economy*, New York: Henry Holt and Co.

Erens, B., Primatesta, P. and Prior, G. (2001) *Health Survey for England 1999: the health of minority ethnic groups*, London: HMSO.

Estes, C., Biggs, S. and Phillipson, C. (2003) *Social Theory, Social Policy and Ageing: a critical introduction*, Buckingham: Open University Press.

Euronet (2000) *Draft Charter of Fundamental Rights of the European Union*, Brussels: 5 June, CHARTE 4343/00 CONTRIB 207, Brussels: Euronet.

Evandrou, M. (1999) Simulating social policy in an AGEing society. Paper given at the annual conference of the British Society of Gerontology, *Tradition and Transition: ageing into the third millennium, 17–19 September*.

Evandrou, M. (2000) Social inequalities in later life: the socioeconomic position of older people from ethnic minority groups in Britain, *Population Trends*, 101, 11–18.

Evandrou, M. and Glaser, K. (2003) Combining work and family life: the pension penalty of caring, *Ageing and Society*, 23, 583–601.

Evandrou, M. and Glaser, K. (2004) Family work and quality of life: changing economic and social roles through the lifecourse, *Ageing and Society*, 24, 771–92.

Evans, G. and Tallis, R. (2001) A new beginning for care for the elderly, *British Medical Journal*, 322, 801–8.

Evers, H. (1985) The frail elderly woman: emergent questions in ageing and women's health, in E. Lewin and V. Olesen (eds) *Women, Health and Healing*, New York: Tavistock.

Felstead, A. and Jewson, N. (2000) *In Work, at Home*, London: Routledge.

Finch, J. (1995) Responsibilities, obligations and commitments, in I. Allen and S. Perkins (eds) *The Future of Family Care for Older People*, London: HMSO.

Finch, J. and Groves, D. (1980) Community care and the family: a case for equal opportunities, *Journal of Social Policy*, 9, 487–511.

Finch, J. and Groves, D. (eds) (1983) *A Labour of Love*, London: Routledge and Kegan Paul.

Finch, J. and Mason, J. (1990) Filial obligations and kin support for elderly people, *Ageing and Society*, 10, 151–73.

Finch, J. and Mason, J. (1993) *Negotiating Family Responsibilities*, London: Routledge.

Finch, J. and Mason, J. (1997) Filial obligations and kin support, in J. Bornat, J. Johnson, C. Pereira, D. Pilgrim and F. Williams (eds) *Community Care: a reader*, 2nd edition, London: Open University Press/Macmillan, 96–106.

Fine, M. and Glendinning, C. (2005) Dependence, independence or inter-dependence? Revisiting the concepts of 'care' and 'dependency', *Ageing and Society*, 25, 601–21.

Finkelstein, V. (1991) Disability: an administrative challenge? The health and welfare heritage, in M. Oliver (ed.) *Social Work, Disabled People and Disabling Environments*, Buckingham: Open University Press.

Finkelstein, V. (1998) The biodynamics of disablement? Paper presented at World Health Organisation *Disability and Rehabilitation Systems, Research Seminar, Harare, Zimbabwe*.

Firth, R. (2006) Learning from overseas social workers' experience in the UK, *Seminar on International Recruitment, King's College London, July*.

Fisher, B. and Tronto, J. (1990) Toward a feminist theory of caring, in E. Abel and M. Nelson (eds) *Circles of Care: work and identity in women's lives*, Albany: State University of New York Press.

Fisher, M. (1994) Man made care: community care and older male carers, *British Journal of Social Work*, 24, 659–68.

Fisher, M., Qureshi, H., Hardyman, W. and Homewood, J. (2006) *Using Qualitative Research in Systematic Reviews: older people's views of hospital discharge*, How knowledge works in social care, Report 9, London: Social Care Institute of Excellence.

Fisk, M. (1997) Telecare equipment in the home: issues of intrusiveness and control, *Journal of Telemedicine and Telecare*, 3, Supplement 1.

Fitzgerald, G. (2006) The realities of elder abuse, in A. Wahidin and M. Cain (eds) *Ageing, Crime and Society*, Cullompton: Willan Publishers, 90–107.

Forder, J., Knapp, M., Hardy, B., Kendall, J., Matosevic, T. and Ware, P. (2004) Prices, contracts and motivations: institutional arrangements in domiciliary services, *Policy and Politics*, 32, 207–22.

Forster, M. (1989) *Have the Men Had Enough?* London: Penguin.

Frankenburg, R. (1966) *Communities in Britain*, London: Penguin.

Fraser, N. (1989) *Unruly Practices: power, discourses and gender in contemporary social theory*, Cambridge: Polity.

Fry, C. (2003) Kinship and supportive environments of aging, in H.-W. Wahl, R. Scheidt and P. Windley (eds) *Annual Review of Gerontology and Geriatrics: Focus on Aging in Context: sociophysical environments*, 23, 313–33.

Garthwaite Report (2005) *Social Work in Wales: a profession to value*, http://www.allwalesunit.gov.uk/index.cfm?articleid=1704.

Gattuso, S. and Bevan, C. (2000) Mother, daughter, patient, nurse: women's emotion work in aged care, *Journal of Advanced Nursing*, 31, 892–9.

Gerrish, K., Husband, C. and Mackenzie, J. (1996) *Nursing for a Multi-ethnic Society*, Buckingham: Open University Press.

Giddens, A. (1990) *The Consequences of Modernity*, Cambridge: Polity.

Gilligan, C. (1982) *In a Different Voice: psychological theory and women's development*, London: Harvard University Press.

Gilligan, C. (1987) Moral orientation and moral development, in E. Feder Kittay and D.T. Meyers (eds) *Women and Moral Theory*, Ottawa: Rowman and Littlefield.

Ginn, J. and Arber, S. (1994) Midlife women's employment and pension entitlement in relation to co-resident adult children in Great Britain, *Journal of Marriage and the Family*, 56, 813–19.

Glendinning, C. and Means, R. (2004) Rearranging the deckchairs on the Titanic of long term care – is organisational integration the answer? *Critical Social Policy*, 24, 435–57.

Goffman, E. (1961) *Asylums: essays on the social situations of mental patients and other inmates*, London: Penguin.

Goulbourne, H. (1999) The transnational character of Caribbean kinship in Britain, in S. McRae (ed.) *Changing Britain: families and households in the 1990s*, Oxford: Oxford University Press, 176–99.

Graham, H. (1983) Caring: a labour of love, in J. Finch and D. Groves (eds) *A Labour of Love*, London: Routledge and Kegan Paul.

Grant, G. (2001) Older people with learning disabilities: health, community inclusion and family caregiving, in M. Nolan, S. Davies and G. Grant (eds) *Working with Older People and Their Families: key issues in policy and practice*, Buckingham: Open University Press.

Grant, G. and Nolan, M. (1993) Informal carers: sources and concomitants of satisfaction, *Health and Social Care in the Community*, 1, 147–59.

Green, D. (1994) Foreword in C. Quest (ed.) *Liberating Women . . . From Modern Feminism*, London: IEA Health and Welfare Unit.

Green, A., Hogarth, T. and Shackleton, R. (1999) *Long Distance Living: dual location households*, Bristol: Policy Press.

Green, H. (1988) *General Household Survey 1985*, London: HMSO.

Griffiths Report (1998) *Community Care: agenda for action*, London: HMSO.

Guardian (2001) Old timers, G2, 30 January 2001.

Guberman, N. and Maheu, P. (1999) Aging and caregiving in ethno cultural families: diverse situations but common issues, in S. Neysmith (ed.) *Critical Issues for Future Social Work Practice with Aging Persons*, New York: Columbia University Press, 127–55.

Gubrium, J.F. (1995) Taking stock, *Qualitative Health Research*, 5, 267–9.

Gunaratnam, Y. (1990) Asian carers, *Carelink*, 11, 6.

Gunaratnam, Y. (1997a) Breaking the silence: black and ethnic minority carers and service provision, in J. Bornat, J. Johnson, C. Pereira, D. Pilgrim and F. Williams (eds) *Community Care: a reader*, 2nd edition, London: Open University Press/ Macmillan, 114–24.

Gunaratnam, Y. (1997b) Culture is not enough: a critique of multiculturalism in palliative care, in D. Field, J. Hockey and N. Small (eds) *Death, Gender and Ethnicity*, London: Routledge, 166–86.

Gunaratnam, Y. (2004) Skin matters: 'race' and care in the health services, in J. Fink (ed.) *Care: personal lives and social policy*, Bristol: The Open University/The Policy Press, 112–41.

Guralnik, V. and Haigh, K. (2002) Learning models of human behaviour with sequential patterns in *AAAI–02 Workshop on Automation as Caregiver: the role of intelligent technology in elder care, Edmonton, Canada, July*, Minneapolis: Honeywell, 24–30.

Habermas, J. (1991) *The Theory of Communicative Action: reason and the rationalization of society*, Cambridge: Polity.

Hancock, R. (1998) Housing wealth, income and financial wealth of older people in Britain, *Ageing and Society*, 18, 5–33.

Hardill, I., Spradbery, J., Arnold-Boakes, J. and Marrugat, M.L. (2005) Severe health and social care issues among British migrants who retire to Spain, *Ageing and Society*, 25, 769–83.

Harrington Meyer, M., Herd, P. and Michel, S. (2000) Introduction, in M. Harrington Meyer (ed.) *Care Work: gender, class and the welfare state*, New York: Routledge.

Heal, S. (1994) *An Introduction to the Issues in Respect of Young Carers*, London: Carers National Association.

Heenan, D. (2000) Informal care in farming families in Northern Ireland: some considerations for social work, *British Journal of Social Work*, 30, 855–66.

Help the Aged (2006) *A Review of Evidence on Quality of Life in Care Homes*, London: Help the Aged in partnership with the National Care Forum and the National Care Homes Research and Development Forum.

Henderson, J. and Forbat, L. (2002) Relationship-based social policy: personal and policy constructions of 'care', *Critical Social Policy*, 22, 669–87.

Hendrick, H. (1994) *Child Welfare: England 1872–1989*, London: Routledge.

Henwood, M. (1995) *Making a Difference? Implementation of the community care reforms two years on*, London: Nuffield Institute/Kings Fund.

Hill, M. (1990) The manifest and latent lessons of child abuse inquiries, *British Journal of Social Work*, 20, 197–213.

Hirdman, Y. (1998) State policy and gender contracts, in E. Drew, R. Emereck and E. Mahon (eds) *Women, Work and the Family in Europe*, London: Routledge, 36–46.

Hochschild, A. (1983) Emotion work, feeling rules and social structure, *American Journal of Sociology*, 85, 551–75.

Holden, C. (2002) British government policy and the concentration of ownership in long-term care provision, *Ageing and Society*, 22, 79–94.

Home Office (1999) *Sure Start*, London: Home Office.

Hood, C., Jones, D., Pidgeon, N. and Turner, B. (1992) Risk management, in Royal Society Study Group (ed.) *Risk Analysis, Perception and Management: report of a Royal Society Study Group*, London: The Royal Society.

hooks, b. (1981) *Ain't I a Woman: black women and feminism*, London: Pluto Press.

Hooyman, N. and Gonyea, J. (1995) *Feminist Perspectives on Family Care: policies for gender justice*, New York: Sage.

Howe, D. (2005) *Child Abuse and Neglect: attachment, development and intervention*, Basingstoke: Palgrave Macmillan.

Hubert, J. (1997) Living arrangements for young adults with learning disabilities, in J. Bornat, J. Johnson, C. Pereira, D. Pilgrim and F. Williams (eds) *Community Care: a reader*, 2nd edition, London: Open University Press/Macmillan.

Hughes, B. (2005) Love's Labours Lost? Feminism, the Disabled People's Movement and an ethic of care, *Sociology*, 39, 259–75.

Hussein, S. and Manthorpe, J. (2005) An international review of the long term care workforce: policies and shortages, *Journal of Aging and Social Policy*, 17, 75–94.

Huxley, P., Evans, S. and Munroe, M. (2006) International recruitment in social care: a systematic review and preliminary evidence. Seminar on *International Recruitment, King's College London, July*.

Jani-Le Bris, H. (1993) *Family Care of Dependent Older People in the European Community*, Dublin: European Foundation for the Improvement of Living and Working Conditions.

Jerrome, D. (1981) The significance of friendships for women in later life, *Ageing and Society*, 1, 175–97.

Johri, M., Beland, F. and Bergman, H. (2003) International experiments in integrated care for the elderly: a synthesis of the evidence, *International Journal of Geriatric Psychiatry*, 18, 222–35.

Jones, G. (2006) Recognising the social and temporal contexts of youth. Seminar on *Children's rights and citizenship, Swansea University, May*.

Jones, G. and Wallace, C. (1992) *Youth, Family and Citizenship*, Buckingham: Open University Press.

Jones, K. (1996) George III and changing views of madness, in J. Heller, J. Reynolds, R. Gomm, R. Muston and S. Pattinson (eds) *Mental Health Matters*, Buckingham: Open University Press.

Jones, K. and Fowles, A.J. (1984) *Ideas on Institutions: analysing the literature on long term care and custody*, London: Routledge and Kegan Paul.

Jones, L. (1998) Changing health care, in A. Brechin, J. Walmsley, J. Katz and S. Peace (eds) *Care Matters: concepts, practice and research in health and social care*, London: Sage, 154–69.

Jones, R. (2006) *Sure Start in Later Life presentation*, London, 26 January.

Joseph, A. and Hallman, B. (1996) Caught in the triangle: the influence of home, work and elder location on work–family balance, *Canadian Journal of Aging*, 15, 393–413.

Joseph, A. and Martin-Matthews, A. (1993) Growing old in aging communities, *Journal of Canadian Studies*, 28, 14–29.

Kahn, R. and Antonucci, T. (1980) Convoys over the life course: attachment roles and social support, in P. Baltes and O. Brim (eds) *Life Span Developments and Behaviour*, Vol. 3, New York: Academic Press.

Karn, V. (1977) *Retiring to the Seaside*, London: Routledge and Kegan Paul.

Katbamna, S., Ahmad, W., Bhakta, P., Baker, R. and Parker, G. (2004) Do they look after their own? Informal support for South Asian carers, *Health and Social Care in the Community*, 12, 398–406.

Katz, R., Daatland, S.O., Lowenstein, A., Bazo, M.T., Ancizu, I., Herlofson, K., Mehlhausen-Hassoen, D. and Prilutzky, D. (2003a) Family norms and preferences in intergenerational relations: a comparative perspective, in V.L. Bengtson and A. Lowenstein (eds) *Global aging and challenges to families*, New York: Aldine de Gruyter, 305–26.

Katz, R., Lowenstein, A., Prilutzky, D. and Mehlhausen-Hassoen, D. (2003b) Intergenerational solidarity, in A. Lowenstein and J. Ogg, *OASIS Final Report*, Haifa, Israel: The Center for Research and Study of Aging, 165–92.

Kauh, T.O. (1997). Intergenerational relations: older Korean-Americans' experiences, *Journal of Cross-Cultural Gerontology*, 12, 245–71.

Kaye, L. and Applegate, J. (1990) *Men as Caregivers to the Elderly*, Lexington, MA: Lexington Books.

Keating, N. and Martin-Matthews, A. (forthcoming) *A Good Place to Grow Old? Critical perspectives on rural ageing*, Bristol: The Policy Press.

Keating, N., Otfinowski, P., Wenger, C., Fast, J. and Derksen, L. (2003) Understanding the caring capacity of informal networks of frail seniors: a case for care networks, *Ageing and Society* Concept Forum, 23, 1, 115–27.

Keating, N. and Phillips, J. (forthcoming) A critical human ecology approach, in N. Keating and A. Martin-Matthews (forthcoming) *A Good Place to Grow Old? Critical perspectives on rural ageing*, Bristol: The Policy Press.

Keeley, B. and Clarke, M. (2002) *Carers Speak Out Project: report on findings and recommendations*, London: The Princess Royal Trust for Carers.

Keeling, S. (2001) Relative distance: ageing in rural New Zealand, *Ageing and Society*, 21, 605–19.

Kemshall, H. (2002) *Risk, Social Policy and Welfare*, Buckingham: Open University Press.

Kemshall, H. and Pritchard, J. (1996) *Good Practice in Risk Assessment and Risk Management*, London: Jessica Kingsley.

Kim, H., Hisata, M., Kai, I. and Lee, S. (2000) Social support exchange and quality of life among the Korean elderly, *Journal of Cross-Cultural Gerontology*, 15, 331–47.

King, R., Warnes, T. and Williams, A. (2000) *Sunset Lives: British retirement migration to the Mediterranean*, Oxford: Berg.

Kittay, E. (1999) *Love's Labour: essays on women, equality and dependency*, New York: Routledge.

Kitwood, T. (1997) *Dementia Reconsidered: the person comes first*, Buckingham: Open University Press.

Knipscheer, C.P.M. (1988) Temporal embeddedness and aging with the multigenerational family: the case of grandparenting, in J.E. Birren and V.L. Bengtson (eds), *Emergent Theories of Aging*, New York: Springer, 426–46.

Kolb, K. (2003) Long distance caregivers and stress. Presentation for the symposium *Caregiving from Afar: Does Geographic Distance Matter? The Gerontological Society of America Conference, November, San Diego*.

Kröger, T. (2001) *Comparative Research on Social Care: the state of the art*, Brussels: European Commission.

La Fromboise, T., Coleman, H. and Gerton, J. (1993) Psychological impact of biculturalism: evidence and theory, *Psychological Bulletin*, 114, 395–412.

Laing and Buisson (2003) *Care of Elderly People: market survey 2003*, 16th edn, London: Laing and Buisson.

Land, H. (1991) Time to care, in M. Maclean and D. Groves (eds) *Women's Issues in Social Policy*, London: Routledge, 7–19.

Land, H. (2002) Spheres of care in the UK: separate and unequal, *Critical Social Policy*, 22, 13–32.

Laws, G. (1997) Spatiality and age relations, in A. Jamieson, S. Harper and C. Victor (eds) *Critical Approaches to Ageing and Later Life*, Buckingham: Open University Press.

Lawton, M.P. (1980) *Environment and Aging*, Belmont, CA: Brooks/Cole.

Lawton, M.P. and L. Nahemow (1973) Ecology of the aging process, in C. Eisdorfer and M.P. Lawton (eds) *Psychology of Adult Development and Aging*, Washington, DC: American Psychology Association, 619–24.

Lees, S. (2002) Gender, ethnicity and vulnerability in young women in local authority care, *British Journal of Social Work*, 32, 907–23.

Lettke, F. and Klein, D. (2003) Methodological issues in assessing ambivalence in intergenerational relations, in K. Pillemer and K. Lüscher (eds) *Intergenerational Ambivalences: new perspectives on parent-child relations in later life*, Contemporary Perspectives in Family Research Vol 4., Oxford: Elsevier Science Ltd, 85–114.

Levin, E., Sinclair, I. and Gorbach, P. (1989) *Families, Services and Confusion in Old Age*, Aldershot: Gower.

Lewis, J. and Meredith, B. (1988) *Daughters Who Care: daughters caring for mothers at home*, London: Routledge.

Ley, D. and Waters, J. (2004) Transnational migration and the geographical imperative, in P. Jackson, P. Crang and C. Dwyer (eds) *Transnational Spaces*, London: Routledge, 104–21.

Lin, G. and Rogerson, P. (1995) Elderly parents and the geographic availability of their adult children, *Research on Aging*, 17, 303–31.

Lingsom, S. (1994) *The Development and Impact of Payments for Care*, INAS-NOTAT 4, Oslo: Institut fur socialforskning.

Lister, R. (1997) *Citizenship: feminist perspectives*, Basingstoke: Macmillan.

Litwin, H. and Auslander, G. (1990) Evaluating informal support, *Evaluation Review*, 14, 42–56.

Lloyd, L. (2004) Mortality and morality: ageing and the ethics of care, *Ageing and Society*, 24, 235–56.

London Borough of Brent (1985) *A Child in Trust: the report of the panel of inquiry into the circumstances surrounding the death of Jasmine Beckford*, London: London Borough of Brent.

Lorenz-Meyer, D. (2003) The ambivalence of parental care among young German adults, in K. Pillemer and K. Lüscher (eds) *Intergenerational Ambivalences: new perspectives on parent–child relations in later life*, Contemporary Perspectives in Family Research Vol 4., Oxford: Elsevier Science Ltd, 225–52.

Lowenstein, A. (2005) Global ageing and challenges to families, in M. Johnson (ed.) *The Cambridge Handbook of Age and Ageing*, Cambridge: Cambridge University Press, 403–13.

Lowenstein, A., Katz, R., Mehlhausen-Hassoen, D. and Prilutzky, D. (2003) *The Research Instruments in the Oasis Project: old age and autonomy, the role of service systems and intergenerational family solidarity*, Haifa, Israel: The Center for Research and Study of Aging, The University of Haifa.

Lüscher, K. (1999). Ambivalence: a key concept for the study of intergenerational relations, in S. Trnka, *Family Issues Between Gender and Generations*. Seminar report, European Observatory on Family Matters, 11–25.

Lüscher, K. (2003) Conceptualising and uncovering intergenerational ambivalence, in K. Pillemer and K. Lüscher (eds) *Intergenerational Ambivalences: new perspectives on parent-child relations in later life*, Contemporary Perspectives in Family Research Vol 4., Oxford: Elsevier Science Ltd, 23–62.

Lüscher, K. and Pillemer, K.A. (1998) Inter-generational ambivalence: a new approach to the study of parent-child relations in
later life, *Journal of Marriage and the Family*, 60, 413–25.

Lymbery, M. (2005) *Social Work with Older People: context,
policy and practice*, London: Sage.

Mand, K. (2006) *Social Capital and Transnational South Asian
Families: rituals, care and provision*, Families and Social Capital
ESRC Research Group Working Paper No. 18, London: South
Bank University.

Mansfield, P. and Collard, J. (1988) *The Beginning of the Rest of
Your Life*, Basingstoke: Macmillan.

Manthorpe, J. (2003) Nearest and dearest? The neglect of lesbians
in caring relationships, *British Journal of Social Work*, 33,
753–8.

Manthorpe, J., Walsh, M., Alaszewski, A. and Harrison,
L. (undated) *Issues of Risk Practice and Welfare in Learning
Disability Services*, Working Papers on Risk and Social
Welfare, paper no. 5, Institute of Health Studies, University of
Hull.

Markides, K.S. and Krause, N. (1985). Intergenerational solidarity
and psychological well being among older Mexican Americans:
a three-generational study, *Journal of Gerontology*, 40,
390–2.

Marshall, V.W., Matthews, S.H. and Rosenthal, C.J. (1993) Elu-
siveness of family life: a challenge for the sociology of aging, in
G.L. Maddox and M.P. Lawton (eds), *Annual Review of Gerontology and Geriatrics: focus on kinship, aging and social
change*, New York: Springer.

Marshall, V., Rosenthal, C.J., and Daciuk, J. (1987) Older parents'
expectations for filial support, *Social Justice Research*, 1, 405–
24.

Martin-Matthews, A. (2007) Situating 'home' at the nexus of the
public and private spheres: aging, gender and home support
work in Canada, in S. Arber, L. Andersson and A. Hoff (eds)
*Gender, Aging and Power: changing dynamics in Western societ-
ies*, Current Sociology: SSIS Monograph (in press).

Martin-Matthews, A. and Mahmood, A. (forthcoming) Boundary
management and relationship issues for home support workers
and home care recipients in Canada, in A. Martin-Matthews and
J. Phillips (eds) *Blurring the Boundaries*, New York: Lawrence
Erlbaum.

Mason, J. (1999) Living away from relatives: kinship and geographical reasoning, in S. McRae (ed.) *Changing Britain: families and households in the 1990s*, Oxford: Oxford University
Press, 156–76.

Massey, D. (1994) *Space, Place and Gender*, Cambridge: Polity.

Massey, D. (2005) *For Space*, London: Sage.

Matthaei, J. (2001) Healing ourselves, healing our economy: paid work, unpaid work and the next stage of feminist economic transformation, *Journal of Radical Political Economics*, 33, 461–94.

May, S. (1999) Critical multiculturalism and the cultural difference: avoiding essentialism, in S. May (ed.) *Cultural Multiculturalism*, London: Falmer Press, 11–41.

Maynard, A. (2000) Rationing care, in A. Warnes, L. Warren and M. Nolan (eds) *Care Services for Later Life*, London: Jessica Kingsley.

McCarthy, H. and Thomas, G. (2004) *Home Alone*, London: Demos.

McEwan, P. and Laverty, S. (1949) *The Chronic Sick and Elderly in Hospital*, Bradford (B) Hospital Management Committee.

McGrother, C., Hauck, A., Bhaumik, S., Thorp, C. and Taub, N. (1996) Community care for adults with learning disability and their carers: needs and outcomes from the Leicester register, *Journal of Intellectual Disability Research*, 40, 183–90.

McKie, L., Gregory, S. and Bowlby, S. (2002) Shadow times: the temporal and spatial frameworks and experiences of caring and working, *Sociology*, 36, 897–924.

McKie, L., Gregory, S. and Bowlby, S. (2004) *Caringscapes: experiences of caring and working*, Centre for Research on Families and Relationships, research briefing, 13 February.

McMullin, J. (1995) Theorising age and gender relations, in S. Arber and J. Ginn (eds) *Connecting Gender and Age*, Buckingham: Open University Press, 30–41.

McPherson, B. (2004) *Aging as a Social Process: Canadian perspectives*, 4th edn, Toronto: Oxford University Press.

Means, R., Richards, S. and Smith, R. (2000) *Community Care Policy and Practice*, Basingstoke: Macmillan.

Means, R., Richards, S. and Smith, R. (2003) *Community Care: Policy and Practice*, 3rd edn, Basingstoke: Palgrave.

Mears, J. and Watson, E. (forthcoming) Boundaries blurred and rigid at the frontline of care: care workers and the negotiation of relationships with the older people they are caring for, in A. Martin-Matthews and J. Phillips (eds) *Blurring the Boundaries*, New York: Lawrence Erlbaum.

Mehta, K. and Thang, L.L. (forthcoming) The dynamics of multi-generational care in Singapore, in A. Martin-Matthews and J. Phillips (eds) *Blurring the Boundaries*, New York: Lawrence Erlbaum.

Miller, E. and Gwynne, G. (1972) *A Life Apart*, London: Tavistock.

Milligan, C. (2003) Location or dislocation? Towards a conceptualisation of people and place in the care-giving experience, *Social and Cultural Geography*, 4, 455–70.

Milligan, C. (2006) Caring for older people in the 21st century: notes from a small island, *Health and Place*, 12, 320–31.

Mir, G. and Tovey, P. (2003) Asian carers' experiences of medical and social care: the case of cerebral palsy, *British Journal of Social Work*, 33, 465–79.

Mitchell, W. and Sloper, P. (2002) *Quality Services for Disabled Children*, York: SPRU.

Mooney, A. and Statham, J. (2002) *To Work or Not? Informal care and work after fifty*, Bristol: Joseph Rowntree Foundation with The Policy Press.

Morgan, P. (1994) Double income, no kids: a case for a family wage, in C. Quest (ed.) *Liberating Women . . . From Modern Feminism*, London, IEA Health and Welfare Unit.

Morioka, K., Sugaya, Y., Okuma, M., Nagayama, A. and Funjii, H. (1985) Intergenerational relations: generational differences and changes, in K. Morioka (ed.) *Family and Life Course of Middle-aged Men*, Tokyo: The Family and Life Course Study Group, 188–217.

Moroney, R. (1976) *The Family and the State: considerations for social policy*, London: Longman.

Morris, J. (1991) *Pride Against Prejudice: transforming attitudes towards disability*, London: The Women's Press.

Morris, J. (1997a) Care or empowerment? A disability rights perspective, *Social Policy and Administration*, 31, 54–60.

Morris, J. (1997b) 'Us' and 'them'? Feminist research and community care, in J. Bornat, J. Johnson, C. Pereira, D. Pilgrim and F. Williams (eds) *Community Care: a reader*, 2nd edition, London: Open University Press/Macmillan, 106–70.

Morrow, V. (1998) *Understanding Families: children's perspectives*, London: National Children's Bureau.

Mörtberg, C. (2000) Information technology and gender: challenges in a new millennium, *Women and the Information Society Conference, Reykjavik, April 14.*

Moss, P. (2003) Getting beyond childcare: reflections on recent policy and future possibilities, in J. Brannen and P. Moss (eds) *Rethinking Children's Care*, Buckingham: Open University Press, 25–43.

Moss, P. and Cameron, C. (2001) *Mapping of Care Services and the Workforce, Care Work in Europe*, http://144.82.31.4/carework/uk/reports/index.htm.

Motel-Klingebiel, A., Tesch-Roemer, C. and von Kondratowitz, H.-J. (2005) Welfare states do not crowd out the family: evidence for mixed responsibility from comparative analysis, *Ageing and Society*, 25, 863–82.

Mulholland, J. (1995) Nursing, humanism and transcultural theory: the 'bracketing out' of reality, *Journal of Advanced Nursing*, 22, 442–9.

Munday, B. (1998) The old and the new: changes in social care in central and Eastern Europe, in B. Munday and G. Lane (eds) *The Old and the New: changes in social care in central and Eastern Europe*, Canterbury: European Institute of Social Services.

Nagel, J. (1994) Constructing ethnicity: creating and recreating ethnic identity and culture, *Social Problems*, 41, 152–76.

Naik, D. (1991) An examination of social work education within an anti-racist framework, *Setting the Context for Change*, Leeds: Central Council for Education and Training in Social Work, 153–65.

Navaroo, V. (2002) Neoliberalism, 'globalization', unemployment, inequalities and the welfare state, in V. Navaroo (ed.) *The Political Economy of Social Inequalities: consequences for health and quality of life*, New York: Baywood Publishing Company, 33–107.

Nazroo, J. (2003) The structuring of ethnic inequalities in health: economic position, racial discrimination and racism, *American Journal of Public Health*, 93, 277–84.

Nazroo, J. (2006) Ethnicity and old age, in J. Vincent, C. Phillipson and M. Downes (eds) *The Futures of Old Age*, London: Sage/British Society of Gerontology, 62–72.

Nazroo, J., Bajekal, M., Blane, D. and Grewal, I. (2004) Ethnic inequalities, in A. Walker and C.H. Hennessy (eds) *Growing Older, Quality of Life in Old Age*, Maidenhead: Open University Press, 35–59.

Neal, M., Chapman, N., Ingersoll-Dayton, B. and Emlen, A. (1993) *Balancing Work and Caregiving for Children, Adults and Elders*, California: Sage.

Neal, M., Hammer, L., Bonn, K. and Lottes, J. (2003) Long distance caregiving among working, sandwiched couples: an exploratory study. Presentation for the symposium *Caregiving from Afar: Does Geographic Distance Matter? The Gerontological Society of America Conference*, November, San Diego.

Netten, A., Darton, R. and Williams, J. (2002) The rate, causes and consequences of home closures, Discussion Paper 1741/2, Personal Social Services Research Unit, University of Kent.

Netten, A., Williams, J. and Darton, R. (2005) Care-home closures in England: causes and implications, *Ageing and Society*, 25, 319–38.

Nippert-Eng, C. (1996) *Home and Work*, Chicago: University of Chicago Press.

Nissel, M. and Bonnerjea, L. (1982) *Family Care of the Handicapped Elderly. Who Pays?* London: Policy Studies Institute, no. 602.

Nolan, M., Grant, G. and Keady, J. (1996) *Understanding Family Care*, Buckingham: Open University Press.

Norman, A. (1985) *Triple Jeopardy: growing old in a second homeland*, Policy Studies in Ageing No. 3, London: Centre for Policy on Ageing.

Oakley, A. (1974) *The Sociology of Housework*, Oxford: Martin Robertson.

Office of the Deputy Prime Minister (2006) *A Sure Start for Later Life: ending inequality for older people*, London: DH, DWP, SEU and ODPM.

Oldman, C. (2003) Deceiving, theorizing and self-justification: a critique of independent living, *Critical Social Policy*, 23, 44–62.

Oliver, M. (1990) *The Politics of Disablement*, Basingstoke: Macmillan.

Oliver, M. (2004) The social model in action: if I had a hammer, in C. Barnes and G. Mercer (eds) *Implementing the Social Model of Disability: theory and research*, Leeds: The Disability Press.

Orme, J. (2001) *Gender and Community Care: social work and social care perspectives*, Basingstoke: Palgrave.

Pahl, R. (2000) *On Friendship*, Cambridge: Polity.

Parker, G. (1985) *With Due Care and Attention*, London: Policy Studies Institute.

Parker, M.W., Call, V.R. and Kosberg, J. (2001) Geographic separation and contact between adult children and their parents. Paper presented at the *IAG 17th World Congress, Vancouver, Canada*.

Parton, C. and Parton, N. (1989) Child protection: the law and dangerousness, in O. Stevenson (ed.) *Child Abuse: public policy and professional practice*, Hemel Hempstead: Harvester Wheatsheaf.

Parton, N. (1985) *The Politics of Child Abuse*, Basingstoke: Macmillan.

Parton, N. (1996) Social work, risk and the 'blaming society', in N. Parton (ed.) *Social Theory, Social Change and Social Work*, London: Routledge.

Parton, N. (2003) Rethinking professional practice: the contributions of social constructionism and the feminist 'ethic of care', *British Journal of Social Work*, 33, 1–16.

Peace, S. (1998) Caring in place, in A. Brechin, J. Walmsley, J. Katz and S. Peace (eds) *Care Matters: concepts, practice and research in health and social care*, London: Sage.

Peace, S., Holland, C. and Kellaher, L. (2006*) Environment and Identity in Later Life*, Buckingham, Open University Press.

Peace, S., Kellaher, L. and Willcocks, D. (1997) *Re-evaluating Residential Care*, Buckingham: Open University Press.

Pearlin, L., Piopli, M. and McLaughlin, A. (2001) Caregiving by adult children: involvement, role disruption and health, in R. Binstock and L. George (eds) *Handbook of Aging and the Social Sciences*, 238–54.

Penhale, B. (2000) Discharge planning, in M. Davies (ed.) *The Blackwell Encyclopaedia of Social Work*, Oxford: Blackwell, 94–6.

Penhale, B. (2002) Social work in health care settings, in M. Davies (ed.) *The Blackwell Companion to Social Work*, Oxford: Blackwell, 235–42.

Penhale, B. (2006) Global developments in relation to elder abuse, in A. Wahidin and M. Cain (eds) *Ageing, Crime and Society*, Cullompton: Willan Publishers.

Phillips Report (1954) *Report of the Committee on the Economic and Financial Problems of the Provision for Old Age*, Cmd 9332, London: HMSO.

Phillips, D., Siu, O.-L., Yeh, A. and Cheng, K. (2005) Ageing and the urban environment, in G. Andrews and D. Phillips (eds) *Ageing and Place: perspectives, policy, practice*, London: Routledge.

Phillips, J. (1989) *Private Residential Care*, Aldershot: Ashgate.

Phillips, J. (1995) Balancing work and care in Britain, in J. Phillips (ed.) *Working Carers*, Aldershot: Avebury, 42–57.

Phillips, J. (2000) Working women: paid and unpaid carers, in M. Bernard, J. Phillips, L. Machin and V. Davies (eds) *Women Ageing: changing identities, challenging myths*, London: Routledge, 40–58.

Phillips, J., Bernard, M. and Chittenden, M. (2002a) *Juggling Work and Care*, Joseph Rowntree Foundation Report, Bristol: Joseph Rowntree Foundation/Policy Press.

Phillips, J., Bernard, M. and Chittenden, M. (2002b) *Juggling Work and Care: the experiences of working carers of older adults*. Unpublished interview transcripts, Keele: Keele University.

Phillips, J., Bernard, M., Phillipson, C. and Ogg, J. (2002) Social support in later life: a study of three areas, *British Journal of Social Work*, 30, 837–54.

Phillips, J., Ogg, J. and Ray, M. (2003) Ambivalence in intergenerational relations, in A. Lowenstein and J. Ogg (eds), *OASIS Final Report*, Haifa: The University of Haifa, Israel, 193–226.

Phillips, J. and Ray, M. (2003) The qualitative phase, in A. Lowenstein and J. Ogg (eds), *OASIS Final Report*, Haifa: The University of Haifa, Israel, 103–26.

Phillips, J., Ray, M. and Marshall, M. (2006) *Social Work with Older People*, Basingstoke: Palgrave.

Phillips, J. and Waterson, J. (2002) Care management and social work: a case study of the role of social work in hospital discharge to residential or nursing home care, *European Journal of Social Work*, 5, 171–86.

Phillipson, C., Alhaq, E., Ullah, S. and Ogg, J. (2000) Bangladeshi families in Bethnal Green, London: older people, ethnicity and social exclusion, in A. Warnes, L. Warren, and M. Nolan (eds) (2000) *Care Services for Later Life: transformations and critiques*, London: Jessica Kingsley, 273–90.

Phillipson, C., Bernard, M., Phillips, J. and Ogg, J. (2001) *The Family and Community Life of Older People*, London: Routledge.

Phillipson, C. and Scharf, T. (2005) *The Impact of Government Policy on Social Exclusion Among Older People*, London: Office of the Deputy Prime Minister, 53–65.

Pickard, L., Wittenberg, R., Comas-Herrera, A., Davies, B. and Darton, R. (2000) Relying on informal care in the new century? Informal care for elderly people in England to 2031, *Ageing and Society*, 20, 745–72.

Pickard, L., Wittenberg, R., Comas-Herrera, A., Davies, B. and Darton, R. (2001) Community care for frail older people: analysis using the 1998/9 General Household Survey, in S. Tester, C. Archibald, C. Rowlings and S. Turner (eds) *Quality in Later Life: rights, rhetoric and reality. Proceedings of the British Society of Gerontology 30th Annual Conference*, Stirling: University of Stirling, 201–6.

Pilcher, J. and Whelan, I. (2004) *50 Key Concepts in Gender Studies*, London: Sage.

Player, S. and Pollock, A. (2001) Long term care: from public responsibility to private good, *Critical Social Policy*, 21, 231–55.

Qureshi, H. and Walker, A. (1989) *The Caring Relationship: elderly people and their families*, Basingstoke: Macmillan.

Report of the Royal Commission on the Care and Control of the Feeble Minded (1908).

Renwick, R. and Brown I. (1996) The Centre for Heath Practitioners: conceptual approach to quality of life – being, belonging and becoming, in R. Renwick, I. Brown and M. Nagler (eds) *Quality of Life in Health Promotion and Rehabilitation: conceptual approaches, issues and applications*, Thousand Oaks, CA: Sage.

Richards, S. (2000) Bridging the divide: elders and the assessment process, *British Journal of Social Work*, 30, 37–49.

Rimmer, L. (1983) The economics of work and care, in J. Finch and D. Groves (eds) *A Labour of Love*, London: Routledge and Kegan Paul.

Ritchie, J. (1994) *The Report of the Inquiry into the Care and Treatment of Christopher Clunis*, London: HMSO.

Rodriguez, J. (1993) *Family Care of the Older Elderly: Spain*, Working Paper No. WP/93/23/EN, Dublin: European Foundation for the Improvement of Living and Working Conditions.

Rose, H. and Bruce, E. (1995) Mutual care but different esteem: caring between older couples, in S. Arber and J. Ginn (eds) *Connecting Gender and Ageing*, Buckingham: Open University Press, 114–28.

Rosenmayr, L. and Köckeis, E. (1963) Propositions for a sociological theory of ageing and the family, *International Social Science Journal*, 15, 410–26.

Rowles, G. (1978) *Prisoners of Space*, Boulder: Westview.

Rowles, G. (2005) What time is this place? The temporal depth of living environments in old age. Presentation at the *Gerontological Society of America Conference, Orlando, November*.

Royal Society (1992) *Risk: analysis, perception and management*, Report of a Royal Society Study group, London: The Royal Society.

Saleeby, D. (1997) *The Strengths Perspective in Social Work Practice*, New York: Longman.

Salvage, A. (1995) *Who Will Care? Future prospects for family care of older people in the European Union*, Dublin: European Foundation for the Improvement of Living and Working Conditions.

Scharf, T., Phillipson, C., Smith, A. and Kingston, P. (2002) *Growing Older in Socially Deprived Areas: social exclusion in later life*, London: Help the Aged.

Schneider, J., Murray, J., Banerjee, S. and Mann, A. (1999) EURO-CARE: a cross-national study of co-resident spouse carers for people with Alzheimer's disease: factors associated with carer burden, *International Journal of Geriatric Psychiatry*, 14, 651–61.

Sevenhuijsen, S. (1998) *Citizenship and the Ethics of Care*, London: Routledge.

Sevenhuijsen, S. (2000) Caring in the third way: the relation between obligation, responsibility and care in Third Way discourse, *Critical Social Policy*, 20, 5–37.

Shakespeare, T. (2000) *Help*, Birmingham: Venture Press.

Shanas, E., Townsend, P., Wedderburn, D., Friis, H., Milhoj, P. and Stehouwer, J. (1968) *Old People in Three Industrial Societies*, London: Routledge and Kegan Paul.

Sheldon, J.H. (1948) *The Social Medicine of Old Age*, Oxford: Oxford University Press.

Silvers, A. (1995) Reconciling equality to difference: caring (f)or justice for people with disabilities, *Hypatia*, 10, 30–55.

Silvers, A. (1997) Reconciling equality to difference: caring f(or) justice for people with disabilities, in P. DiQuinzo and I. Young (eds) *Feminist Ethics and Social Policy*, Bloomington: Indiana University Press.

Sin, C.H. (2006) Expectations of support among white British and Asian-Indian older people in Britain: the interdependence of formal and informal spheres, *Health and Social Care in the Community*, 14, 215–24.

Sixsmith, A. (1986) The meaning of home: an exploratory study of environmental experience, *Journal of Environmental Experience*, 6, 281–98.

Social Care Institute of Excellence (2005) *Developing Social Care: the current position*, London: SCIE.

Staffordshire County Council (1991) *The Pindown Experience and the Protection of Children*, Stafford: Staffordshire County Council.

Stone, D. (2000a) Caring by the book, in M. Harrington Meyer (ed.) *Care Work*, New York: Routledge, 89–111.

Stone, D. (2000b) Why we need a care movement, *The Nation*, 13 March, 13–15.

Stone, R. and Wiener, J. (2001) *Who Will Care For Us? Addressing the long term care workforce crisis*, Washington, DC: The Urban Institute and the American Association of Homes and Services for the Aging.

Sutherland Report (1999) *With Respect to Old Age: long term care – rights and responsibilities*: A Report by the Commission on Long Term Care, Cm 4192–I, London: HMSO.

Taint, G., Thompson, P., Winfield, H. and Simmons, D. (2002) *Paying for Care Handbook*, Child Poverty Action Group, www.cpag.org.uk.

Taylor, C. and White, S. (2000) *Practising Reflexivity in Health and Welfare: making knowledge*, Buckingham: Open University Press.

Taylor, P. and Parrot, J. (1988) Elderly offenders, *British Journal of Psychiatry*, 152, 340–6.

Tennstedt, S., McKinlay, J. and Sullivan, L. (1989) Informal care for frail elders: the role of secondary caregivers, *The Gerontologist*, 29, 677–83.

Thoburn, J. (2000) Outcomes for children of minority ethnic origin placed with adoptive or permanent foster families, *Improving Outcomes in Family Placement: Expectations and Experiences Baaf Research Symposium, 29 November*.

Thoburn, J., Chand, A. and Procter, J. (2004) *Child Welfare Services for Minority Ethnic Families: the research reviewed*, London: Jessica Kingsley.

Thomas, T. and Wall, G. (1993) Investigating older people who commit crime, *Elders: Journal of Care and Practice*, 2, 53–60.

Thompson, A. (1949) Problems of ageing and chronic sickness (1), *British Medical Journal*, 30 July, 250.

Tierney, A., Worth, A., Closs, S., King, C. and Macmillan, M. (1994) Older patients' experiences of discharge from hospital, *Nursing Times*, 90, 36–9.

Tobin, S. (1996) A non-normative old age contrast: elderly parents caring for offspring with mental retardation, in V.L. Bengtson (ed.) *Adulthood and Ageing: research on continuities and discontinuities*, New York: Springer.

Townsend, P. (1957) *The Family Life of Old People*, London: Routledge and Kegan Paul.

Townsend, P. (1962) *The Last Refuge*, London: Routledge and Kegan Paul.

Tronto, J. (1993) *Moral Boundaries: a political argument for an ethic of care*, New York: Routledge.

Tudor Hart, J. (1971) The inverse care law, *The Lancet*, 1, 406–12.

Tweed, C. and Quigley, G. (1999) Some ethical considerations of dwelling-based telecare systems for the elderly. Working paper, School of Architecture, The Queen's University of Belfast.

Twigg, J. (1997) Deconstructing the 'Social Bath': help with bathing at home for older and disabled people, *Journal of Social Policy*, 26, 211–32.

Twigg, J. (1998) Informal care, in M. Bernard and J. Phillips (eds) *The Social Policy of Old Age*, London: Centre for Policy on Ageing, 128–41.

Twigg, J. (2001) *Bathing – The Body and Community Care*, London: Routledge.

Twigg, J. and Atkin, K. (1994) *Carers Perceived: policy and practice in informal care*, Buckingham: Open University Press.

Ungerson, C. (1987) *Policy is Personal: sex, gender and informal care*, London: Tavistock.

Ungerson, C. (1995) Gender, cash and informal care: European perspectives, *Journal of Social Policy*, 24, 31–52.

Ungerson, C. (2000) Cash in care, in M. Harrington Meyer (ed.) *Care Work: gender, class and the welfare state*. New York: Routledge, 68–88.

Ungerson, C. (2004) Whose empowerment and independence? A cross-national perspective on 'cash for care' schemes, *Ageing and Society*, 24, 189–221.

Ungerson, C. and Kember, M. (1997) *Women and Social Policy: a reader*, London: Macmillan.

Van Groenou, M. and van Tilburg, T. (2003) Network size and support in old age: differentials by socio-economic status in childhood and adulthood, *Ageing and Society*, 23, 625–45.

van Tilburg, T. (1998) Losing and gaining in old age: changes in personal network size and social support in a four-year longitudinal study, *Journal of Gerontology: Social Sciences*, 53B, 6, S313–S323.

Vaughan-Morgan, J., Maude, A. and Thompson, K. (1952) *The Care of Older People*, London: Conservative Political Centre.

Victor, C., Bowling, A., Bond, J. and Scambler, S. (2005) Loneliness, social isolation and living alone in later life, http://www.growingolder.group.shef.ac.uk/ChristinaVictor.htm.

Wærness, K. (1992) On the rationality of caring, in A. Showstack Sassoon (ed.) *Women and the State*, London: Routledge.

Wagner, D. (2003) Research on long-distance caregivers: what we (don't) know. Presentation for the symposium *Caregiving from Afar: Does Geographic Distance Matter? The Gerontological Society of America Conference, November, San Diego*.

Waine, B., Tunstill, J. and Meadows, P. with Peel, M. (2005) *Developing Social Care: values and principles*, London: Social Care Institute of Excellence.

Walker, A. (1993) *Age and Attitudes*, Brussels: EC Commission.

Walker, A. and Ahmad, W. (1994) Windows of opportunity in rotting frames: care providers' perspectives on community care and black communities, *Critical Social Policy*, 40, 46–69.

Walker, A. and Phillipson, C. (1986) Introduction, in C. Phillipson and A. Walker (eds) *Ageing and Social Policy: a critical assessment*, Guildford: Gower.

Walmsley, J. (1996) Doing what mum wants me to do: looking at family relationships from the point of view of adults with intellectual disabilities, *Journal of Applied Research in Intellectual Disabilities*, 9, 324–41.

Walsh, M., Alaszewski, A., Harrison, L. and Manthorpe, J. (undated) National policies and official reports and inquiries concerning child welfare and the care of adults with learning disabilities – a brief historical review. Working Papers on Risk and Social Welfare, paper No. 11, Institute of Health Studies, University of Hull.

Wanless, D. (2006) Social care needs and outcomes. A background paper for the Wanless Social Care Review, July 2005.

Ward, H. (1995) *Looking After Children: research into practice*, London: HMSO.

Ward, H. and Rose, W. (eds) (2002) *Approaches to Needs Assessment in Children's Services*, London: Jessica Kingsley.

Ward-Griffin, C. (forthcoming) Health professionals caring for aging relatives: a professional or personal issue? in A. Martin-Matthews and J. Phillips (eds) *Blurring the Boundaries*, New York: Lawrence Erlbaum.

Warnes, A. (1992) Migration and the lifecourse, in A. Champion and A. Fielding (eds) *Migration Processes and Patterns Volume 1. Research Progress and Prospects*, London: Belhaven, 175–87.

Warnes, A. (2006) Surrey Conference on *Home Care Transition, July, Surrey University*.

Warnes, T. and Ford, R. (1995) Migration and family care, in I. Allen and E. Perkins (eds) *The Future of Family Care for Older People*, London: HMSO.

Wasserman, S. and Galaskiewicz, J. (eds) (1994) *Advances in Social Network Analysis: research in the social and behavioural sciences*, Thousand Oaks, CA: Sage.

Watson, N., McKie, L., Hughes, B., Hopkins, D. and Gregory, S. (2004) (Inter)Dependence, needs and care: the potential for disability and feminist theorists to develop an emancipatory model, *Sociology*, 38, 331–50.

Weinberg, A., Williamson, J., Challis, D. and Hughes, J. (2003) What do care managers do? A study of working practices in older people's services, *British Journal of Social Work*, 33, 901–19.

Webb, S. (2001) Some considerations on the validity of evidence based practice in social work, *British Journal of Social Work*, 31, 57–79.

Welsh Assembly Government (2006) *Fulfilled Lives, Supportive Communities*, Cardiff: Welsh Assembly Government.

Wendell, S. (1996) *The Rejected Body: feminist and philosophical reflections on disability*, London: Routledge.

Wenger, C. and Jingming, L. (1999) Support networks in Beijing (China) and Liverpool (UK): differences and similarities, *Hallym International Journal of Aging*, 1, 46–57.

Wenger, G.C. and Keating, N. (forthcoming) The evolution of networks of rural older adults, in N. Keating and A. Martin-Matthews (eds) *A Good Place to Grow Old? Critical perspectives on rural ageing*, Bristol: The Policy Press.

White, A. (2002) *Social Focus in Brief: ethnicity 2002*, London: ONS.

Wiles, J. (2003) Daily geographies of care-givers, *Social Science and Medicine* 57, 1307–25.

Williams, A. (1997) Rationing health care by age: the case for, *British Medical Journal*, 314, 820–2.

Williams, F. (1995) Race/ethnicity, gender and class in welfare states: a framework for comparative analysis, *Social Politics*, 2, 2.

Williams, F. (1997) Care: anthology, in J. Bornat, J. Johnson, C. Pereira, D. Pilgrim and F. Williams (eds) *Community Care: a reader*, London: Open University Press and Macmillan, 81–95.

Williams, F. (2000) Travels with nanny, destination good enough. A personal/intellectual journey through the welfare state, Inaugural Lecture, University of Leeds, May 11, www.leeds.ac.uk/sociology.

Williams, F. (2001) In and beyond New Labour: towards a new political ethics of care, *Critical Social Policy*, 21, 467–93.

Williams, F. (2004) *Rethinking Families*, London: Calouste Gulbenkian Foundation.

Williams, F. (2005) Intersecting issues of gender, 'race' and migration in the changing care regimes of UK, Sweden and Spain. Paper presented at the *Annual Conference of International Sociological Conference Research Committee 19, September 8–10, North-Western University, Chicago*.

Willmott, P. and Young, M. (1957) *Family and Class in a London Suburb*, London: Routledge and Kegan Paul.

Wistow, G. (2005) *Developing Social Care: the past, the present and the future*, London: Social Care Institute of Excellence.

Wistow, G., Knapp, M., Hardy, B., Forder, J., Kendall, J. and Manning, R. (1996) *Social Care Markets: progress and prospects*, Buckingham: Open University Press.

Wolf, D. and Longino, C. (2005). Our 'increasingly mobile society'? The curious persistence of a false belief, *The Gerontologist*, 45, 5–11.

Wolfensberger, W. (1980) A brief overview of the principle of normalization, in R. Flynn and K. Nitsch (eds) *Normalization, Social Integration and Community Services*, Baltimore: University Park Press.

Women's Royal Volunteer Service (2004) Society must challenge loneliness and save lives, press release, 8 March.

Wright, F. (1986) *Left to Care Alone*, Aldershot: Gower.

Young, M. and Willmott, P. (1957) *Family and Kinship in East London*, London: Routledge and Kegan Paul.

Index